AN ANXIOUS SPRING

AN ANXIOUS SPRING

New and Selected Poems
1980–2022

JOHN LEVETT

All rights reserved. No part of this work covered by the copyright herein may be reproduced or used in any means – graphic, electronic, or mechanical, including copying, recording, taping, or information storage and retrieval systems – without written permission of the publisher.

Printed by imprintdigital
Upton Pyne, Exeter
www.digital.imprint.co.uk

Typesetting and cover design by The Book Typesetters
hello@thebooktypesetters.com
07422 598 168
www.thebooktypesetters.com

Published by Shoestring Press
19 Devonshire Avenue, Beeston, Nottingham, NG9 1BS
(0115) 925 1827
www.shoestringpress.co.uk

First published 2022
© Copyright: John Levett

The moral right of the author has been asserted.

ISBN 978-1-915553-13-3

ACKNOWLEDGEMENTS

Grateful thanks to John Lucas at Shoestring Press and the late Harry Chambers at Peterloo Poets for publishing my six previous collections from which this book is predominantly derived.

My thanks also to the editors of the following anthologies in which a number of the these poems appeared:

The Arvon Foundation Anthology 1982, *The Poetry Book Society Anthology 1989–1990* (Hutchinson), *The Orange Dove of Fiji* (Hutchinson) 1989, *The Forward Book of Poetry 1993*, *Scanning the Century* (Viking Penguin) 1999, *Poems of the Decade* (Forward) 2001, *The Twentieth Century in Poetry* (Ebury Press) 2011, *The Hippocrates Book of the Heart* 2017, *Strike Up The Band* (Plas Gwyn Books) 2017.

Grateful acknowledgements to the following magazines and newspapers where some of these poems were first published:

Critical Survey, *Encounter*, *The Frogmore Papers*, *The Guardian*, *The Honest Ulsterman*, *The Interpreter's House*, *The Literary Review*, *London Magazine*, *London Review of Books*, *Magma*, *The New Statesman*, *The North*, *Orbis*, *Outposts*, *Oxford Poetry*, *Poetry Durham*, *Poetry Mattters*, *PN Review*, *Poetry Review*, *Prospice*, *Raceme*, *The Reader*, *The Rialto*, *Smiths Knoll*, *The Spectator*, *Times Literary Supplement*, *The Warwick Review* and to *New Poetry* first broadcast on BBC Radio 3.

Thanks are also due to the organizers and judges of the following competitions: Stroud, Bridport, Yorkshire, Ware, Kent & Sussex and the National Poetry Competition.

Thank you also to the judges of the New Statesman Prudence Farmer Award 1982 and the Whitbread Poetry Prize 1994.

For Wendy, Ruth and Peter

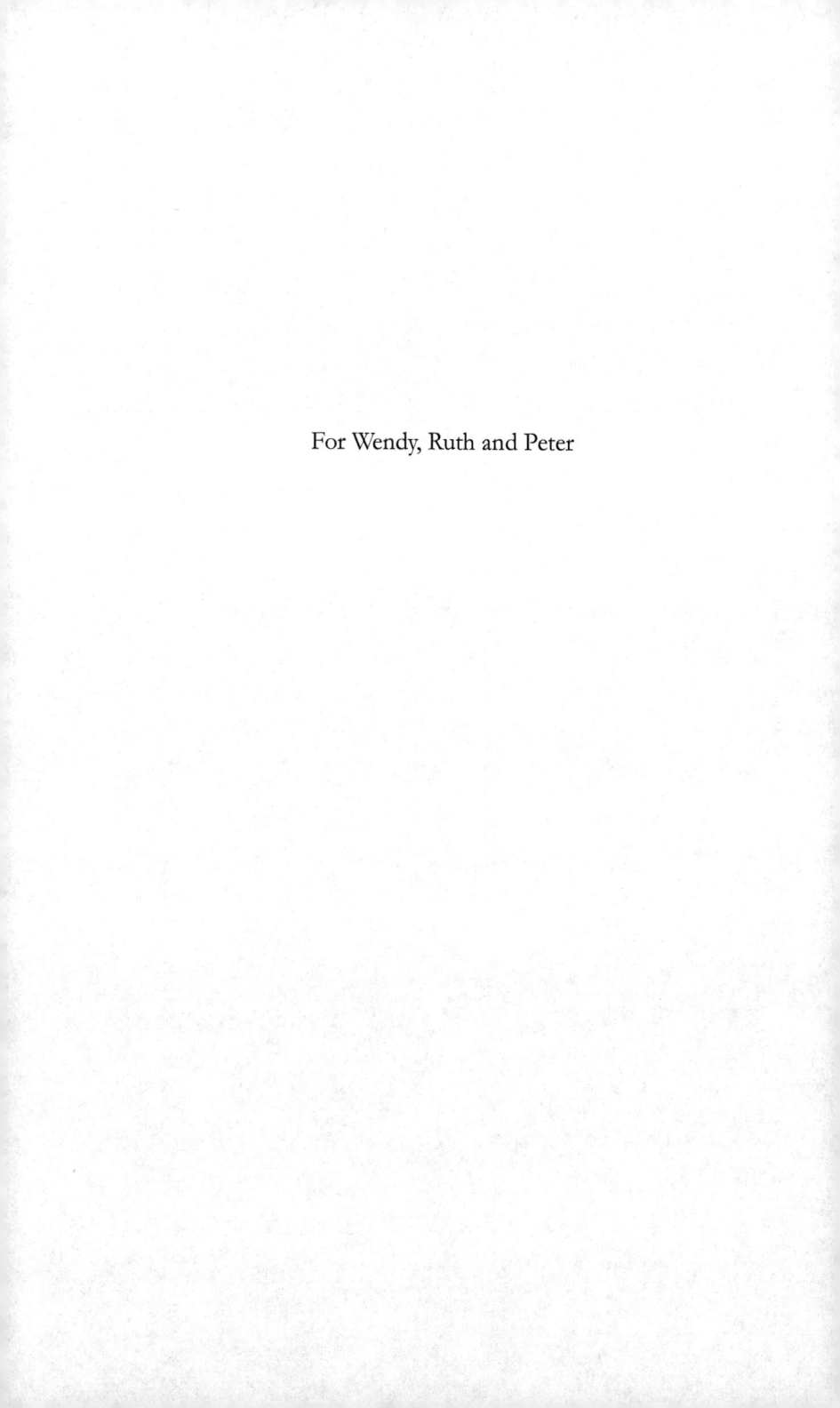

CONTENTS

Changing Sides

The Insect House	3
A Year	4
The Photographs of Paris	5
Open Day	6
A Letter from My Aunts	7
Whistlers	8
Repairs	9

Skedaddle

A Piece of Cake	13
SDI	14
Los Angeles 1984	16
Bunker	17
The Bridge at Avignon	18
Agoraphobia	19
A Departure	20
Skedaddle	21
Old Holborn	23
The Ghost of Blériot	24
Jack-in-a-Box	25
Radiotherapy	26
Anniversary	27
Piano	28
Closing Time	29
Sprinters	30
The Snow Globe	31
Packed Lunches	32
Laughter	33
Here Be Dragons	35

Their Perfect Lives

Am	39
The Gas Mask	40
A Shrunken Head	41
Pomegranate	42
Zebra	43
A Slip	45
A Long Shot	46
Pluto's Fist	47
The Butterfly Centre	48
Steps	49
Heirloom	50
Singeing	51
Airfix	52
Early Warning	53
Vacuum	55
X-Ray	56

A Short History of Mornings

A Fork	59
Lemons	60
Leatherjackets at Dusk	61
Gentlemen	62
Magnesium	63
The Adder's Skin	64
Copper Falls	65
A Small Disorderly Song	66
Taking Pains	67
The Weight of Everything	68
Harmonica	69
The Magnifying Glass	70
Greensleeves	71
Salix Contorta	72
Snowdrops	73
A Crystal Skull	74
The Crack	75

Sea Song	76
Tourniquets	77
Doodle	78
Lemonade	79
A Glass Neck	80
Signal Failure	81
Silver	82
Ammonite	83
Mud in Her Eye	84
A Pretty Kettle of Fish	85
Devilsbit	86
Matthew Smith	87
Pillion	88
Blackspot	89
A Slight Delay	90
A Short History of Mornings	91
Tippex	92
An Idle Bask	93

The Nick of Time

The Ice House	97
The Holly Leaf	98
Sexing Skeletons	100
Water Boatman	101
Paperweight	102
Imperial Leather	103
Glacier Mints	105
Beatrice Cenci	106
Obsequies	108
Triangle	109
Stylus	110
Floc	111
Understudy	112
The Afterlives of the Anarchists	113
A Difference of Opinion	114
Bluebell	115
Radium	116

Glass Ceiling	117
Cheers	118

A Song About You

Lunula	121
Trombicula	122
The Age of Steam	123
Silver Mist	124
Woman in Blue	126
Fisheye	127
On the Possibilty of Recycling Gold from the Mouths of the Dead	128
Dead Man's Fingers	129
A Cardboard Witch	130
Witch Hazel	131
Cold Shoulder	132
Escapology	133
Scooter	135
A Pair of Boots	136
Yes	137

New Poems

The White Sparrow	141
Hindsight	142
Tomfoolery	143
At First I Failed	144
Lifebuoy	145
A Million of Repentence	147
Hydrangeas	149
Ötzi	150
Roués	151
On a Balcony Falling	152
One for Sorrow	153
Greengage	154
Anopheles	155

A Late Christening	156
Snowball	157
Mute	158
Iodine	159
Shoo	160
Chin Up	161
Singalong	162
Clock & Thistle	163
In a Nutshell	164
Oyster Thief	165

From

Changing Sides

Peterloo Poets

1983

THE INSECT HOUSE

This artificial darkness is more real
Than any country midnight. One by one
Attendants throw the switches that reveal
The glass walls of each tank, an Asian moon,
And taped along the violet edge
Of warm, exhaustive privilege
The thermostats displayed like silver spoons.

Inside this careful landscape of placed stones
And salt-white sticks the insects are at large,
We listen for the click of absent bones,
Watch for dissimulation, camouflage;
Beyond our vision movement lies
Immured in motionless disguise
And folded in unguessable montage.

Kafka-like each wing case and each husk
Emerges from the body of the scene,
Folds back again as moist, electric dusk
Bathes each vagrant gesture in a clean,
Receptive, almost milk white coat
That purifies yet leaves remote
The surface of each fitful, lifting seam.

Your palm damp in my palm, about to leave
This base line of existence, we're aware
Of how the shifting twilight can revive
These introverted privacies of fear;
We flicker darkly on the glass
And brighten into sudden mass
And flare as sunlight shoulders through the door.

A YEAR

Last autumn, planting bulbs, we saw her laugh
Unguardedly, not knowing we had heard;
Around her hair the breeze had wound its scarf,
Beneath her feet next summer lay interred.

Through winter, living fifteen doors away,
And touched by his unreason she became
Strindbergian, a play within a play,
Alternately renewed by guilt and blame.

Her death that spring found all the street prepared,
She turned her back on backs already turned,
The crocus bulbs and daffodils still flared
And petered out, but after she had burned.

The garden goes on slowly through the year,
The rubber gloves she used to plant and cut
Hang dimly in the porch and evenings wear
Their fingers lightly as the lamps come out.

THE PHOTOGRAPHS OF PARIS

She spreads them out and shows them one by one,
Their photographs of Paris, how they lean
From left to right beneath a tilting sun
So near the edge it could be me or you
Surrendering the foreground to the scene
And poised as if to demonstrate the view.

The city holds the centre and they pose
With nominal correctness to record
Their shifting presence, only to dispose
Of any doubts they later entertain
As to the truth of memory abroad
Worn soft by years of having to remain.

The clichés of the Tuileries collect
In Kodachrome across a three inch square,
The other shots, all much as we'd expect,
The Champs de Mars, Montmartre, Notre Dame,
The distance speared upon the Eiffel Tower,
The porticos, impressive, without name.

Unchanging, it's as if the years will change,
Or somehow their small camera reinvent
The whole idea of Paris, making strange
The permanence and newness of the place,
A process that turns into ornament
The smile upon each half familiar face.

OPEN DAY

The children have made globefish from balloons
And moulded coloured paper, thread and pin,
Fat schools of them now swarm the afternoon
Along the sunlit corridor and turn
In notional directions to begin
Each static voyage, each pointed, slow return.

We file into the classroom, write our names
In yellow chalk upon the coarsened board
And seriously cross the floor to claim
A tiny chair, a table-top, knee high,
While all the time behind us fly this hoard
Of buoyant fish that mock such gravity.

Around the walls are pictures of our pasts,
Simple, subtle fictions, one word keys,
Mummy, Daddy, Shopping, lives recast,
The truth perhaps, unstylish, rendered down
To such a scale it forces our unease,
Out on a limb, self-conscious, overgrown.

Each child's report, each conference in low tones
Is tangible to please or disappoint;
Are these the gifts and weaknesses one owns?
A frieze of random pixies, scattered elves
Droops low above our heads as we await
Unwelcome verdicts, hold them to ourselves.

Today, by some rare chance, we top the class,
Our daughter wins approval; now restored
We rise to go, feel guilty as we pass,
And burdened as we are by this new sense
Forget the downdraft from the open door
That lifts the fish, makes waves, is excellence.

A LETTER FROM MY AUNTS

Now, as always, money involved and love
Reiterated clumsily in lines
That cannot hold a parallel but move
And tentatively vary on each page;
A crookedness that relishes confines,
The thickening infirmities of age.

We mean so much to all of them; our lives,
Their insubstantial details, have become
The certain forms from which their own derive.
There is no sense of distance, only years
Between our house and their disarming home:
We are, they say, so often in their prayers.

Two generations. Countryside and town.
Such vague gaps of assumption now divide
Their kind interpretations and our own,
And all my letters back appear as crude,
False essays in sincerity beside
Their gentle and unearned solicitude.

Exposed to guilt I read it through once more,
Surprised again how innocent and shy
Old fashioned words of tenderness still are,
Like echoes of the schoolroom where they claim
That eloquence beyond vocabulary,
The tiny kiss, the star beside each name.

WHISTLERS

So many nights, so many different blues,
Such morning underwater, so much mist,
Such lucent tracks of stars, arpeggios
Of miles that turn to inches on the wrist.
What little warmth there is must crackle through
The hollow silks, the kneaded amethyst.
Beneath the lake his brush has thrown a fuse.
Abstraction, then, can be as cold as this.

Beneath the smart remarks the tinted smoke,
The gestural epiphany, the feint
From right to left, the held and softened stroke
Articulate, not *gossiping in paint*,
Yet somehow anecdotal, like a joke
Exacting the responses of a saint.

REPAIRS

Your needle pulls blue thread across
White sleeves to underline
How small domestic purposes
Grow quickly serpentine,

And plunges through the stiffened waves
Of cotton to redress
The way this vague June light behaves,
Corrosive idleness.

Your fluent, quick, unknowing flow
Insistently denies
The frown that comes and goes as though
Each stitch were a surprise,

And catches on a broken line
The bracelet of the cuff
In rhythms that at once define
And tell the moments off.

Across the gathered fabric now
The light begins to die
As though the many years to go
Slipped through the needle's eye,

As though your careful hands repair
With all the words I twist
And all the broken things we share
This stitching at my wrist.

From

Skedaddle

Peterloo Poets

1987

A PIECE OF CAKE

I came home late to find you gone,
The party over, floor swept clean,
Wet crockery stacked on its side,
Each good intention magnified.
The hard-edged kitchen hummed and shone;
Quite nakedly along their bone
A pork chop and a lamb chop lay
Among the shrink wrapped canapés,
While mirrored in obsessive squares
A bowl of barely balanced pears
Leaned forward and colluded in
Each seperable brown and green.
That isolated wedge of cake,
So self-contained I thought it fake,
Stood on the fridge and could have been
A Hockney or a late Soutine;
Its thin, acrylic stripe of jam
And matted cells of sponge became
All heightened fact, transfused detail,
Distinctly and absurdly real.
I turned to see your simple note,
The empty hook that held your coat,
Your fragile gift, the washing up,
Each saucer on each gleaming cup,
And propped against reflective tiles
Your rings and contraceptive pills.
All summer I had wondered how
Exactly we had got that far,
And now I think of how you are,
Your finger's tell-tale band of skin
That each warm day is darkening.

SDI

Ten miles above the tits at St Tropez
A satellite's remote, panoptic eye
Is tracking us and quietly waiting for
The gesture that could culminate in war;
You scratch your nose, I finish my ice cream
And screw the silver paper in the sand.
Your milky skin is tanning like a dream.
That ultra-violet shadow is my hand.
The camera rolls on, its frozen lens
Picks out the agriculture of the Fens
Then swaps the filters for the infra-red
Cupolas of beleaguered Leningrad.

You shift and turn, your shoulder-blade could be
The smooth lid on some high-tech armoury
And fear stirs in the craters that begin
To open on my weakly bearded chin.
White clouds wind like a turban round the peaks
That top the Himalayas, and the sun,
Its compost of alchemical techniques,
Transmutes the globe and lets us focus on
Calcutta pullulating with its poor,
The psychopaths that bleed El Salvador,
The human tides of Tokyo and then
The terrifying silence of Phnom Penh.

The earth speeds up, its shrunken polar caps
Like parachutes tumescently collapse,
The tilting coasts of snow give way to ice
Then bergs of light on Asian belts of rice.
At eight you plan to have the hotel fix
Your hair and come to meet me in the town,
Its chill and its salinity that pricks

And tightens up a skin that's nicely brown:
Those stars we hope to drink beneath tonight
Are pledged to North America, their light
An Ice Age brilliance turning even now
The obsolescent hardware of the Plough.

LOS ANGELES 1984

Miniaturized on Astroturf
The golden athletes jump and run
As rolling static breaks like surf
Across the saturated screen;
A mythic Californian sun
Boosting the colour, burns unseen.

In Greenwich, London, heavy rain
Has come to nothing. On the Thames
A tug hoots to an empty crane,
And for as far as the eye can see
The wharves with their defective names
Litter the estuary.

Tonight, like every other night,
Out through the cold and back,
A microelectric satellite
Dodges the stars and reconnects
The unphased image with the docks'
Bronchitic sound effects,

While Coliseums, white and clean,
Stuck in their cubes of coastal haze,
Their tides and fogs of gasoline,
Are bounced across the hyperspace
And only the speed of light delays
The smile on each miniature winner's face.

This is our future, this is why
Remote, evangelistic, bright
America is riding high
On space-wars, sport and politics,
And all the things that won't go right
That a little cash can fix.

BUNKER

Day breaks and the night steams North,
Its pitch dark barges heading for
Cape Rigor and the Land of Truth,
Perfection's speculative glare;
The seas ice over and preserve
Their endlessly refractive coast,
An empty and eternal curve,
Light packed against the polar frost.

These august nights are nothing more
Than souped-up evenings, sweat-soaked sheets,
Or coming to on someone's floor
And morning's featherweight retreats;
And even when we die we live
Hopped up in someone's latest suit,
Pumped full of sour preservative,
Our grin set at the absolute,
For several sticky nights at least
Until we're spaded in or burn
And flames or worms or poltergeist
Snap down the lid on our return.

No wonder, then, we keep this place,
This ideal arctic of the mind,
Depsite the latest U.S. base
Or half-crazed men returning blind;
No wonder that we make it white
And pure and blank, untrespassed on,
And outside time, an infinite
Bright bunker of our own.

THE BRIDGE AT AVIGNON

They are dancing on the bridge at Avignon
In their Flemish clothes and clogs as good as new,
You can see their footwork flicker in the sun,
The river's almost sedimentary glow,

And from their eyes you know they are possessed,
Imprisoned by the tinkling of a tune,
Beside themselves and strangely overdressed
On this cataleptic summer afternoon.

They are dancing and the bridge is made of stone,
The silence is hypnotic and the sky
Is blue above the delta of the Rhône
Where the ancient, sunlit currents multiply.

But no one looks and no one really cares,
The antipopes, the prostitutes, the thieves,
The cripples with their questionable wares,
The retrospective flourish of the trees

Whose dusty branches let the sunlight fall
Then hold it just this inch above the ground
Where the medieval future seems to stall
And the little song goes round and round and round.

AGORAPHOBIA

Here comes the wind with a cloud on its arm
Waltzing high over these acres of warm
Pasture and stubble and joining the trees
In their spirited choreographies.

How should we greet it? Is raising a hat
Considered uncivil on broadlands or flat
Levels of meadow that fold up to where
The shape of a hill makes the wood disappear?

Surely it's spotted us, lifted above
The details of trivial landscape by love
And joined to each other by hands that have grown,
Under the weather, a lattice of bone.

Fear takes you from me like straw on the wind,
The old and abandoned nest of the mind
Goes scattering over promiscuous weald.
Sunshine. Your back's inappropriate shield.

A DEPARTURE

On this mild island even rocks'
Slow tolerance cannot ignore
The humped and unassertive shapes
Of gunboats anchored off the shore.
Now only changing weathers bring
New prospects or some second glance;
A damaged cliff face altering
October's sharp exuberance,
The slack commotion of a sea
Withdrawing as each fumbled wave
Claps out into transparency
Not even sunlight can retrieve.
Departing tourists stand in line,
The ferry sidles to and fro,
Its decks awash, a submarine
Goes down and all our futures go
With what she carries, ordnance, lives,
Partitions of recycled air,
Our stockpiles and preservatives
Submerged and heading God knows where.

SKEDADDLE

It is midnight and I have let in the cat.
I stand at the door and examine the stars
And his shadow skedaddles between my feet,
His Egyptian head and four white paws
Joining me in the cosmic sweep,
The ritualistic goodnight sniff,
Our sense of eternity on the cheap,
The infinite held like a handkerchief.
The moon goes bowling through the air
On its desolate, elliptic spree,
And I watch as its sodium craters flare
From Crises to Tranquility,
From the Sea of Clouds to the Sea of Rains,
From the tumble of one dull red star
To the starboard light of a late night plane
For Archangel or Panama,
Cresting the atmospheric storms
With its TV sets and embargoed arms
And the whole technological can of worms.
Implausibly collapsing star
We, like you, are waiting for
Whatever political key unlocks
Pandora's thermonuclear box,
That Freud, Saussure and Levi-Straus,
Gorbachev and Mickey Mouse,
Islam and the Catholic Church
All join hands as the planets lurch,
And Ptolemy's error and Pascal's doubt,
And the earth and its complicated crust
Will all, like us, go sputtering out
In a puff of unenlightened dust.
A radar dish picks up a breeze,
Black lupins wave beside the gate
Where a clump of Thyme and Japanese
Miniatures proliferate.
I close the door and shoot the bolt

And fork the meat into the bowl.
In caves of ice the currents jolt,
The cryogenic fossils howl
For the quick release, the coming heat
No private life can sublimate.
Slowly, in the dark, I climb the stairs,
Undress and slide beside you into bed
And when I stir your pressure reassures,
You turn and find my shoulder with your head,
Then roll away, convinced that I am there,
That asking any more would be absurd.

OLD HOLBORN

Adrift in suburban gardens
High peonies balloon,
The martin and the jay rehearse
Their thiry-first of June,

Clematis threads its argument
On trellises of blue,
The bald-faced moon ashamedly
Slips down the avenue

As six o'clock evaporates
And pond weeds coil and choke,
And dogged grass perks up again,
And monkey puzzles smoke.

Beyond the shouldered labyrinth
Of crescent, close and lane,
The cinder clicks its fingers,
The wind dives down each drain,

And plexiglass and chromium
Encode a fitful sun,
A futility of signals,
A desolate dry run.

With pinks and flags the cityscape's
Perimeters are trim,
But certainties, like heavy men,
Make chances seem so slim,

As one stands by his window-box
And hangs this bluish net
Above the match that shakes to light
His dodgy cigarette.

THE GHOST OF BLÉRIOT

It isn't the rain but the theory of rain,
The idea, not the particular storm,
The concept of bubbles that brightens champagne,
The mist thrown off not the bottle grown warm;
The unheralded ache in your jaw as the talk
Twists off into her involuntary yawn;
The cul-de-sac on the untaken walk
After the party that leads into dawn.
Exploring the streets in that mildest of Mays,
Preoccupied and inexplicably lost,
Pinched by a chill that would turn to a haze
When the sun was up and the heat came off,
It wasn't the grass but the image of grass,
The picture of smoke not the smoke itself,
The philosophy of the unblown glass
As she reached for the mirrors repetitive shelf,
And the drink unpoured and the words unsaid
And the meeting postponed that would never take place
And the irony of the unmade bed
In the muffed readjustment of her face.
It is not what we know, or think we know,
But the things of which we are never aware
That lead us from where we mean to go
To the town where we finally reappear
With a cloud like the ghost of Blériot
Bumping over the square.

JACK-IN-A-BOX

Shut up, coiled in a compact box
And tethered by an anxious spring,
On call until her hand unlocks
The hinge of my astonishing,
It is for her sake that I keep
Each stunning and advertant leap
Contained so that she may not guess
The force of my preparedness.

My forehead lined and knapped with fear,
Eyes wide with coarse expectancy,
Bestowing on the atmosphere
Whatever she would wish of me,
I am the shock she can't resist,
The leering exhibitionist,
The inexpensive, useful toy
Not even boredom can destroy.

She grows away from me but fright
Will bring her back and terror keep
Her eyes fixed on my stark delight
Emerging from the traps of sleep;
My simple mechanism will
Go with her as a principle
And even when it's broken stay,
With luck, to keep her company.

RADIOTHERAPY

A soft and endless loop
Of fifties music plays
Above our random group;
Well used to these delays
The tropical, lit fish,
Absorbed and pliant, move.
The name tag on your wrist
Has isolated love.
Distraction comes too soon,
They draw lines on your breast,
Or where it once had been,
And usher you, poor guest,
Onto the corridor
Past cupboards, telephones,
Just one of many more
In functional white gowns;
Yet once inside that room
Layed out, marked up, you are
Alone, a long way from
All help and all desire.
Nowadays, thank god, the staff
Have microphones, TVs.
They chat to you and laugh.
Life's little ironies.

ANNIVERSARY

Discarded petals, cabbage whites
Fall past our ears to celebrate
Like gravity's drunk acolytes
Impossibilities of weight.

Our daughter is concerned, our son
Delighted by this sudden brush
With butterflies that one by one
Tip outwards from their startled bush

And clutter our intended stay
So thick upon the air we must
Retread the tar of mid-July
And paddle palms to readjust.

What's panic but a strict surprise?
That blemished wedding picture where
We duck as thin confetti flies
And snows across the camera.

PIANO

We never heard it play, although we knew,
Like so much else it had seen better days,
Had known a lighter touch than we could show,
Been peddled as an instrument of praise;
Had lifted someone's parlour clean above
Their dingily Victorian concerns,
Disconsolate with moonlight, sick with love,
Impassioned and uproarious by turns.
Our front room proved its final resting place,
Untended on the cold linoleum,
A monument to disappointed grace,
A casualty, its gloomy kingdom come.
We broke it up one winter afternoon
With long, unweildly hammers and a saw,
Enjoyed it too, the sudden bearing down
On all that had been sacrosanct before;
The polished top, the pale, discoloured keys,
The unexpected patternings of wire,
Sweet music and its sad redundancies
Cut down to size and ready for the fire.
Three weeks it took to burn and every night
A little more was picked up with the coal
Or balanced on the paper in the grate
To crack and spit abruptly down the scale.
The legs we saved till last, their stubborn fuel
Was resinous, reluctant, slicked with tar,
The lions carved on them motionless until
The downdraft took them upwards with a roar.

CLOSING TIME

Tables of fake onyx,
These flames that mist the cold
Idle gin and tonics
Ungloved hands will hold,
Sifts of fox and coney,
This surplus gleam of brass
Isolate entirely
Our lower-middle-class.

Outside, light-years away
From unattended cars,
December nights display
Expensive looking stars;
Inhuman opulence,
Celestial estates:
Deep, deep inside the Gents
The damp accumulates.

How did we get this far?
The luminous saloon
Holds steady on a tar
That rocks beneath the moon;
Our footprints as we go
Are taken by the frost
Then dusted by the snow
Then covered up and lost.

SPRINTERS

It is spring and the sprinters are out again.
From my window I watch them sample the grass,
Neurotically stepping as though to contain
Whatever it is that makes people fast,
And limbering over the asphalt square
And rocking from foot to colourful foot,
Obsessed with speed, or at least the idea
Of speed's unachievable absolute.
To be honest, they're not really very good,
They are ragged, critically overweight,
And when they start trying their actions are crude,
Their expressions a little too desperate,
And something about them, perhaps this vain,
This repeated, impulsive attempt at speed,
Is suggestive, now it is spring again,
Of all clumsily handled need.

THE SNOW GLOBE

A sudden rise of twee
And gyroscopic snow
Makes hay of gravity
Then settles to a slow

And fitful sediment
That leaves the water clear
To artfully present
Undamaged atmosphere.

Two Grenadiers on guard
Beside a palace gate
Who, motionless, absurd,
Can only stand and wait,

A plastic version of
That old Romantic turn,
The lives that cannot move
Traced round a Grecian urn,

But scaled down for the age
And mass-produced to give
Our minds that lack the range
Some cheap alternative.

Invested with a weight
Beyond their substance these
Lost figures concentrate
A gift's desire to please

With each slow-motion spree
Of decorative snow,
A wished catastrophe
Before the real ones blow.

PACKED LUNCHES

At one o'clock their tiny plastic chairs
Are stacked into the corners of the hall;
Brown apple cores, dead yoghurts, fibrous pears,
Like fall-out from some harvest festival,
All scattered arbitrarily between
These ectoplasmic balls of cellophane.

Their lunch boxes are colourful and stuck
With pictures of Darth Vader, Charlie Brown,
With Snoopy in the doghouse, Donald Duck,
And Jedi in a blaze of silicone;
They tremble on their hinges or fall off,
Indignant ghosts of bright, adhesive fluff.

No space trips for their owners, no escapes,
No lighting out for some deserted star,
And trapped within their own instinctive shapes,
How gravely burdened, vulnerable they are
These sullen, antiseptic Aprils when
Grey cloud reflects the playground's bitumen.

Why Jimmy left an orange, why Yvonne
Had snapped her water biscuit into three,
Why Susan shared her chocolate with John
But John would not share his with Rosemary;
Such mild enigmas surface and half-form
And tease us in the muddle of this room
With all the little treacheries to come.

LAUGHTER

Their voices uncontrolled,
Their sunburned muscles hard
Against the grey and gold
Of beach and promenade,
The local youngsters drift
Through light that interests
This boy's abandoned shirt,
That girl's inventive breasts.

At thirty comes the fear
That negligence is lost;
Our bodies start to wear
Each posture like a cast,
Discretion brings its cramp
And dignity its fuss
To little shifts that vamp
The once spontaneous.

My children thread and turn
Through shuttled waves, or dance
On spindles of the sun
As bigger tides advance,
While I remain composed
In shadow on a chair,
My adolescence closed,
My dreams in ill-repair,
And gracelessly resist
This sudden need to have
Some reason to exist,
Some formulary of love.

I hug a can of beer
And lean towards the light,
Soft puffs of clouds adhere,
Taut surfaces invite;

Against the grey and gold
Of beach and promenade
Down steps the sounds unfold,
Through walls the voices fade
And smaller talk invests
And nods and smiles divert
Those inattentive breasts,
That white, abandoned shirt.

HERE BE DRAGONS

Those soft and fat-cheeked cherubim
That blow the clouds across the maps
And stir the seas where islands swim
And into which the cliffs collapse,
Have given up the ghost it seems,
The ragged corners of their world
Are crumpled into browns and creams
Where incredulity lies furled.

Here be dragons. Well, its true,
Surviving our accepted science;
Beneath the sky's commercial blue,
Its bright flags of convenience,
A sea cow or a celeocanth
Is netted by a rusty ship
And shimmies off its beauty with
A bloodless and convulsive flip.

We live in a resilient age.
Caught in a squall of acid rain
Curved isobars describe a cage
Barometers and screens maintain;
Vague distances no longer blur
And superstitions won't unleash
Those legends that with Mercator
Lie beached on shelves of microfiche.

On Lizard Point a five year old
Looks down with a seraphic grin,
Her hair a charitable gold
Of dark, barbaric origin;
She puffs and shreds a dandelion,
A minor wonder, while below,
Caught lightly on the seeds' decline
Obedient, the white yachts go.

From

Their Perfect Lives

Peterloo Poets

1994

AM

The slightest words define the most.
Am, for instance, filling up a life,
Expressing, if expression is compelled,
The body's territorial extent;
Assertion's power to concentrate
A colony of egos in
Their dusty settlements of skin.
Denials, deprecations, steppings down,
Apologies like mornings, wry with mist,
Assumptions of uniqueness, leaky dawns,
Fluorescent, repetitious afternoons,
And fragile nights with sprays of stars,
Each chip and bit, each lucid smithereen,
A glimpse inside what might have been,
A looking glass of overripe
And tinily declarative
Boltholes
Speckled with defections and
Disfigured with this spreading black
That takes each thinning drift of breath
And will not give it back.

THE GAS MASK

Its foetid tubes outlasted usefulness,
War issue circa 1939.
She let me put it on. No one would guess
The skull that filled the rubber snout was mine.
My voice, sucked down into the past decade
Through pipes and perished mouldings, sounded wrong,
Too hollow, other-worldly, too betrayed;
The noise I'd make if I had not been born.
The eyepieces were yellow, pickled cracks
Zigzagged into a musty nasal cave,
A shelter from the senseless dawn attacks
Of guilt and fear if I dared misbehave.
Anonymous I'd prowl the scullery,
Visit every room, patrol the stairs,
Sealed off from mustard gas and Zyklon B,
Dive-bombing beds, napalming rocking chairs.
The mirror in the hallway trapped my shape,
Half a face, a trunk, two rolling eyes,
The blind stare of some technocratic ape
At high-octane liana in the skies.
It grew too hot. My head stewed in my breath,
A sapping, unhygienic foetal bath;
I fought myself and died rehearsing death
Still trapped inside a face that couldn't laugh.
There comes a time when all pretending stops,
The door is opened, out you go to play,
You grab your mask, your bag of acid drops,
Then run and duck towards the grainy day.

A SHRUNKEN HEAD

He's been stitched up, two gummed, black-threaded eyes
Squint back across the decades in surprise
Through spiteful chinks of sunlight, acrid smoke,
Screwed up against some wicked tribal joke.
His rictus has been sewn into a smile,
A tight-lipped dandy puckered into style,
The clearing where his grisly fame began
Still broods beneath the kinks of wood-stained tan.
Flayed leather now, his features smoked and cured,
His niche in culture gruesomely secured,
The needled grin is fixed, drawn back and set
Bone-dry in its reflective cabinet.
A hundred years ago he strayed alone
Towards this room of ritual skin and bone,
Believed in spirits, drank, was secretive
With knives and fish-hooks, dreamed his seed would live,
Sheathed his penis, sweated half the night
On invocations, prayed, prepared to fight,
And felt, perhaps, the moon's leaf-parted shine
Move up his legs and bathe his severed spine;
His head hacked off, half-baked into this face
That swings and grins inside its airless case.
Hung up, he seems to twitch at each dropped word,
As if, although we whisper, he had heard,
And stares through us to what we cannot see,
Our unstitched smiles, their pale atrocity.

POMEGRANATE

My grandmother had cut the thing in half
Then halves again, exposures we could share;
Each slice still glows, a neural photograph,
Uncovered membranes shimmer in cold air.
Aladdin's nightlights. Phoney power cells
In viral cubes so red they almost throb.
Interiorities. A shine that swells.
The first bloom on the neurosurgeon's swab.
That such an uninspired, lacklustre fruit
Could have this deranged beauty stashed inside;
The morning's ultra-red, hymenal loot
An optical surprise solidified.
I hid some pips inside my money-box,
Spoof jewellery that withered overnight;
Now after thirty years a morning rocks
This foetus bathed in dehydrated light.
Packed down into the bright squares of her shawl
She wets her lips and breaks into a grin.
Her white teeth slip; inflamed and glacial
The damaged gums beneath are glistening.

ZEBRA

One sniff would fur the throat,
Immobilize the tongue,
Sponge down the larynx, coat
The windpipe and the lung.
Its potency was caught
On fans of palsied air,
The morning a retort
That trembled over fire,
The curtain of cooked crêpe
And warm, narcotic steam,
Its lyrical escape
From hyperactive flame,
Or bronchial ascent
Above dim ropes and cones,
Night's heavy fender bent
By sodium's splintered bones.

First blacks then whites then blacks
The coarse strips alternate
Between the punched knick-knacks
Of aluminium plate,
Fish bowls of orange light
That flicker on their posts;
Look right, look left, look right,
A litany of ghosts.
In April he was killed;
They laid this down by May.
Municipally willed
He blinks there to this day
But cannot comprehend
His empty seat and desk,
Why, when he raised his hand,
The teacher never asked;

His pile of dust-filmed books,
Each bright, adhesive star
That lit his run towards
This whiff of burning tar.

A SLIP

The foothills of a cloudless sky
Have humped and powdered into dunes,
Their blue-flecked beaches treasured by
Half-buried cups, cheap tablespoons.
The washboard's slope of frosted spars
Swaps lathers as its glassed suds stream,
Pricked rainbows, soap-shagged reservoirs,
Pinked eyelids in a head of steam.
My mother's touch is rough, beneath
The scrubbed band of her wedding ring
A faint red itch, a rash so brief
It flares without her noticing:
The smoky party, drinks, a kiss
That sucked her through a locked back door
Past bundled coats, down stairs to this
Chilled basement's disinfected floor.
A slip. The foetus came and went
One dank, convected Friday night,
Left nothing but detergent, scent,
Sharp cheekbones pocketing the light.
Time bleaches. Buttons plink and dry,
Cuffs wobble round their airless drum
Where whites and cottons flap and sigh
And gather for her hands to come.

A LONG SHOT
for Peter

Lacking a dice my ingenious son
Has made a frail, six-sided paper one.
An irregular cube, its hunkered shape
Is sealed with twelve collars of Sellotape
And decorated with twenty-one dots
Like orbital, lunar forget-me-nots.
He throws the dice for five, I roll a three
Astonished by its botched geometry,
Its bobbled spin, its solo hit and run
Through house dust turned galactic in the sun.
It lands askew, he gets down on his knees
To focus on the inked astronomies
And breathes in very slowly to address
This momentary perch of randomness;
Our carpet and our sofa that maroons
The hindered odds on six blue paper moons.

PLUTO'S FIST

My transfers never took, or not for long,
Saliva and cheap art work peeling off
Or breaking on her saturated tongue
To flecks of Pluto's fist and Popeye's nose,
Acrylic tea leaves, pointillistic froth,
Capillaries, pores doped with cellulose.

Her film of spit would glisten and then thin,
Exasperated colour basked and cooled
On tender strips of visionary skin;
She'd pull the tissue back and slowly tease
A fuzzy likeness, outlines crudely tooled
And proofed against out gobbed transparencies.

That term she met a boy with fake tattoos,
Mauve hearts, barbed arrows peircing LOVE and MUM,
A seethe of hypodermic reds and blues
That hung around all evening like bad news
And left, beneath a scent of bubblegum,
The ultra-violet rumour of a bruise.

THE BUTTERFLY CENTRE
for Ruth

Too pretty by half their chalks and flicked inks
Lift-off from gravel and circle the plants,
Up to their bright, barometric high-jinks,
Dodging down drinkable flightpaths of chance
To customize sunshine, flicker and lurch,
Vamp and soft-pedal, cant over and skim;
Taut, narcissistic, outspread to research
Each dickering paint chart's unfixable whim.

Tranquillized lilacs, regressions of gold,
Haunted manillas and shoaled, nitrous blues,
Skeletal lemons, quick lacings of mould
Swallowtails sew by your black canvas shoes.
Their hand woven gimmicks tickle the air
Grazing from pad to ephemeral pad
And leapfrogging ferns that scaffold the glare
To touch down on netting's trembled brocade.

Distracted you turn and crane over the pond
Where gnats refuel above urinous rocks
And crapulous goldfish decay with their blond
Submarine passions, your dazzled white socks
Stepping from childhood and onto a brink,
Steadied for something more solid and real
Than promises lit by these papery winks
Or the heat that inherits their vanished appeal.

STEPS

A warm pool, one blue flight
Laid flush into the stone,
Her foot's adhesive print,
The padded smudge of bone,
The white gap where her arch
Shrank back, the wave and feint
Of temperatures that parch
The damp's unstable paint.

All day the glass was fogged.
I watched her husband's eyes,
Suspicion waterlogged
Or sunk with ironies;
Her shadow's glossy bake
Stretched out across the grip
Of tiles that turned opaque
Like salt to crust her hip.

Last week he hit her twice
So now she simply sits
And tips and breaks the ice
Indifferently to bits;
Her blouse has come adrift,
Her footprints, as they dry,
Grow tinier and lift
Their body like a sigh.

HEIRLOOM

His skin, a lustrous plastic in its case,
Is dry, too dry to ever leap again
Or surface in that dank, midge-ridden race
Recycled by decades of stippling rain.
The evenings made an heirloom of his eye,
Firelit, inquisitorial, agape,
It glazed with antique memories, the fly,
The rod and line, the hook's barbaric shape,
And clouded with the turmoil of the catch,
The varnished scales articulate to feel
The whack and thrash, the taut, repeated snatch
And plunge that fed the epileptic reel;
The mist of resignation as it dried,
Not guessing in the chilled slump to the net
At life to come shut in this rarefied,
Blue-backed, fern-tangled, airtight cabinet.
The fisherman is dead. His sons are dead,
And their sons too, time's casual defeats;
A haemorrhage, some cancers, suicide,
Closed hospitals, a maze of bombed-out streets:
And still the pike lurks sideways in his gloom,
The tarnish of that flinching, sunlit day
Refloated as the lamplight in our room
Is tilted into dusk and pours away.

SINGEING

The barber's tubes and rubber bulbs,
their wheezing scents, asthmatic talcs,
have long since perished
with the rest of his tribal paraphernalia;
the Brylcreams set in misty jars
and the almost medieval singeing straws,
wax tapers with their red-hot buds
that, smoking, sealed the ends of hairs
and left the neck an acrid stem,
smart meat, a stook of tendons.
They don't go in for singeing now,
hair-triggered, charred against the grain,
the kind of shock reserved for cancers
or to rustle the brain cells of the clinically depressed;
but once its smell
hung over the entire country,
particularly the short-back-and-sides of Southern England,
and especially in the autumn in the shaved afternoons.
Some still believe it works
and some of those
itch to be able to prophesy its return,
that after the harvest, between smashed street lamps,
they might lift up their heads and smell the stubble burn.

AIRFIX

I used to buy a model once a week
With plastic wings on burrs attached to sticks.
I very quickly mastered the technique.
A way of killing time for 2/6d.

At weekends it was something else to do;
Ejector seats, the roundel transfer slips,
Transparent cockpits, surplus films of glue
Like shiny scales beneath my fingertips.

I finished and suspended them from thread
To climb or dive or simulate a swoop,
With one ambitious kit above my bed
Tip-tiltedly prepared to loop-the-loop;

But pretty soon my bedroom had become
An air controller's nightmare, fluff and dust,
The sky above a timeless aerodrome
And waking up a reflex of distrust.

I shelled them with hot pokers and set light
To port and starboard engines, watched them blaze
And smashed them in a parody of flight.
Two dozen hits in half as many days.

They went up like a prayer, a plume of black,
Tiger Moths, Mosquitoes, Yorks and Spits,
And left me with the stench, the lifelong knack
Of posthumously sweeping up the bits.

EARLY WARNING

If you were a nuclear superpower
And I were a buffer state
I'd cling like dirt to your arable skirt
Where the Cruise proliferate,
And my Early Warning system
Would mesh with the nerve ends of yours
And your arms would keep the peace while I sleep
And colonize the stars;
I would launder inflationary taxes
And absorb your acid rain
Though each river and stream might audibly scream
With the ecological pain.

If you were an overgrown continent
And I were a bit on the side
I would love to explore your coastal floor
And the plains where your praries ride.
I would hoover your latest missiles
And polish the stainless steel screens
Where titanium fits like silicone tits
On the tops of your submarines;
And at the United Nations,
Alone in the hullabaloo,
Despite the disgrace and the loss of face
I would always vote for you.

Or if I were the dominant planet
And you were my satellite
I would let you pass through my volatile gas
And spin you through the night:
I would catch and recycle your atoms
And cherish your orbit and shape
The darkened half of your crooked path
To speed up your escape,

And then dance you across the heavens
And blister the firmament
And the stars would uncross at whatever the cost
Until our love was spent.

If I were as rich as you're pretty
Or you were as small as I'm poor
Our hands might have stopped the glandular clock
And the hormonal calendar
Where the season was always autumn
And the weather in bad repair,
Trust hung by a thread and the lights went dead
In your eyes and your blinding hair
As I looked for a private conclusion
Or an easier way to choke
On the gorgeous mess of its loveliness
Before the morning broke.

VACUUM

I came home from the hospital half-stoned
and brushed against your plastic flask
caught cold in a tubular moonlight
falling through a haze of frosted glass.
I stood and watched its wobble of reproach,
the stem of the vacuum silver with absence,
its clinical brightness darkened by tea;
old tensions and
their watermarked fragility
sterilized and shrinking from my touch.

The tube broke with an atmospheric crunch.
I picked it up and shook it.
The noise it made was the same as the sea's
splintered at the chalk foot of a cliff;
a shining insulation,
the mirrored hiss
as microscopic voices seethed
with stillborn cries
and, running through my fingers, were released.

X-RAY

A pearl bulb floods what's left of life,
Its lifted rib-cage streams with light,
The latch of each candescent tooth
Shut on the darkness of your bite;
Its milky, ultra-violet spine
Occluded by a cloudy lung
And, rooted in the skull's blind shine,
The swallowed shadow of your tongue.

These cameras dispense with skin,
Wipe out smudged lipstick, sweat, cologne,
Come down on you and zero in
On deep, illuminated bone,
Ignoring what I thought was real,
Flared nostrils, make-up's high-pitched bloom,
Your instep's rucked, elastic chill,
Tubed breasts and ointments, stale perfume.

They filed your case-notes when you died,
Red ink, sun-faded carbons, tape,
This exposed plate slipped half inside
A tied and humped manilla shape;
Out of the black and unlit blue
Your faint bones glimmer, pale, ill-starred,
Their ghostly edges breaking through
The dog-ears of your record card.

From

A Short History of Mornings

Shoestring Press

2009

A FORK

"I want" she said, taking her tray with the plastic cutlery,
"one blazingly clear yet spaciously rural choice,
a broken white line down an asphalt lane,
its signpost a green wooden fork
on a 90° day,
one path leading up past hen-coops,
through dusty olive groves
to the vinegary sting of inexplicable misery,
the other coasting erratically downhill
through watercress beds and riparian farms,
their network of rivers turned silver with ten thousand fish,
through a trellis hung with garlic and peppers
slap-bang into unspeakable happiness,
the sort you know you will never deserve,
even", she said, leaving a long pause after the "even"
to gobble the last of her *salade niçoise*,
"even when you arrive."

LEMONS

One winter term, back home from school,
I took a matchstick dipped in lemon juice,
wrote a cursive message in the dusk
and held it up to the bleach of light,
watching the ascorbic flow
shine briefly with a love-sick glow
and dry back into paper
as two sash-windows, gathering dark,
faded just above the watermark.
Later, with the lamp switched on,
a fire lit in the grate,
I sneaked up close and held my thin sheet out,
saw the letters mottle one by one,
tortoiseshell on pokerwork
crisped and furled into a phrase:
This is a secret message.
No one must know.
I love you.
After an acid week or two
I got browned off or just outgrew
the need to write to her invisibly,
but hearing today
that she died last year
from cancer in Australia
find hidden in the wreckless scent of lemons,
their burning groves, their tangled thirstiness,
their stained and singed lost blistering of letters,
a zest her bitten thumbnails still release.

LEATHERJACKETS AT DUSK

Already deep into forgetfulness
he kept his foolscap diaries,
sequences of black-ruled weeks,
their moons filling and emptying,
their festivals and feast-days sailing past
with spent half-crowns for bulbs and seeds,
lines for the weather,
vegetables, flowers, names.

"Leatherjackets at dusk",
rising, I suppose, in Folly Lane
above the sloped allotments,
the tar-paper roofs of their huts,
in that softly urban moment
before the lamps come on
when gaiety and joy
are tossed up with dozens
of wire-thin legs and wings
intensely refusing to fall to bits,
meeting and parting in mid-air,
scrabbling with apprehension
and brought down to earth in his spidery scrawl.

Here on the page after forty years,
in wait for the night that did not fall,
are his crash-landed words swept up to tell
anyone who might want to know
how, when the dark is on the backs
of us practical, leather-elbowed chaps,
we scribble.

GENTLEMEN

Glaze-winged urinals mothballed in blue air
Are flushed out of mortar by dusk to reveal
How the spirit of hygiene once cubicled here
Has waited for 85 years to exhale,

As the cowls, pipes and vents of a late afternoon
Break up with ceramics, crashed masonry,
Smashed sinks shining out like chunks of the moon
Through the cathode-ray tube of the CCTV,

With its masked rubber cabling, its infra-red lens
Burning to catch in compressed black and white
The gas mantled ghosts of the gentlemen
Leglessly picking their way into night

Past dark Portakabins, blown by cold rain
Over the car park, the precinct, the mall,
Across hop fields and cliff tops to shake out again
At Arras, Verdun, Cambrai, Passchendaele.

MAGNESIUM

It might as well be gaslight now
That soughs and pouches through the trees,
Lost pockets of foxed sepia,
The silver, pollen-haunted sneeze
Of sunshine and magnesium
Caught in the filter of her veil,
Uplifted faces drained and dumb,
Each smile a failing chemical
That hovers in the nitrate's mist
Where moth-like cousins, lunar aunts
In gauze and satin gloves persist
Through acid-eaten radiance.

There will be mustard gas, morphine,
Candescent flashbacks, shell-burst skies,
Iron lamps whose phutterings sustain
Blown corpses' phosphorescent sighs,
But in the soft hiss of this flare
Time stops to oxidize his face,
Shakes out behind her carboned stare
Annihilations of white lace,
As light implodes and leaves a husk,
A stiff, wing-collared, dried-up glow
Still holding back the brim of dusk
Where all their shining futures go.

THE ADDER'S SKIN
for Fred Dennis

A desiccated trophy in its box
        With snapped clay pipes,
Pink dentures and a dried-out fountain pen,
The memory of its swarthiness unlocks
These sinister, ophidian
        Black lozenges and stripes
That slithered through a fossilizing world
Its bringing out so vividly uncurled.

He'd stunned and slit it, leaving just the flesh,
        The serpentine
Remains dumped in a coil the heat dispelled,
Then stretched its skin like patched-up battledress
On crowds of soldiers as they swelled,
        Assembling line by line
Long trails that in the twinkling of an eye
Snaked all the way to Mons and Picardy;

Then went himself, sloughed off his fifteen years
        To make his mark
And join his brother dead somewhere in France
And where, somehow, a small god interferes
To gas him, give him one last chance
        To shovel through the dark
Snapped shut inside this box where no stray flare
Can pinpoint what the adder's scales oustare.

He'd lift it gently, test its brittle weight,
        Explaining why
When taking life you're best to save its skin
And so let toxic stillness fascinate
Long after any normal perishing,
        Long after each clear eye
Cold rain and clouds of chlorine turned opaque
Had chilled into the dead skin of this snake.

COPPER FALLS

No one I knew ever came out ahead,
Not even my cousin, who prowled the arcade,
Pushing his luck with loose change as he fed
Each shunt and the fistfuls of coins it delayed,
Snake-belted, white knuckled, kissing the edge
Of pennies that wobbled, rolled and fell flat
To shove a bronze fortune nearer the ledge
Of the crazily balanced cash ziggurat.

He'd case the machines, guaging how things would fall,
And weigh up each slot like a connoisseur,
Black plimsoled, short trousered, pre-decimal,
He stares out of snaps in a Box Brownie blur,
Then, fifty years later, seven months dead,
Floats on the shine of my bedside alarm
To signal somehow, although nothing is said,
That a girl jinxed our run with her unlucky charm,

And then, for some reason, both of us smile
At our heap of pooled winnings impulsively lost,
Our spun heads or tails that can't reconcile
The way things fell out to the coins that we tossed,
As night, just once more, lets him use the delay
To search through his pockets and offer to swap
These luminous hours he's been waiting to play
For the second I take for the penny to drop.

A SMALL DISORDERLY SONG

One broken note flew up,
The other ran around
The sound
        Made by a cup
Struck by your tiny fork
And twice showed how the thing
Could sing
        But never talk.
For cracked things that belong
There is no need to speak
They leak
        Hollow with song
And, ringingly moonstruck,
Send laughter into space,
Embrace
        The world's good luck;
As every father charts
The things he will not yet
Regret
        But knows by heart,
And every mother brings
With pain and fear and guilt
The tilt
        In crooked things.
But once, by being young,
You were the everything
We sing
        Or would have sung.

TAKING PAINS
for Peter

All this pink and blue is by my son
And my eyes adore what his hands have done,
Their unsolicited, ravishing, bright
Assurance in each brushstroke taking flight
And taking pains, as painstaking as love
Arriving to give craftsmanship a shove,
And, hanging on the blankness of our wall,
Is what we mean when we say *beautiful*;
And raging at the heart of all this paint
Is the fierce desire to dwell, to reacquaint
The momentary stillness of the eye
With bursts of sun-torn blossom on blue sky.

How little do we think when we shoehorn
With carrycots and buggies our newborn
Into the tightly fitting worlds we shape
How astonishing will be their slow escape
And how the vestiges of what they were
Will linger like a visionary blur;
How nothing can prepare us for the man
Who comes as only revelation can
And shrugs out of this canvas to assume
The coat of light that fills our living room.

THE WEIGHT OF EVERYTHING
for Ruth

Last night I dreamt you taught me how to fly,
Use balance and compression to displace
And push my heaviness into a sky,
Its moon and stars pinpointing my shocked face,

As you had once compressed yourself to swing
Between our lifted arms where you first met
And kicked against the weight of everything
With dangling arabesque and pirouette;

And now, like you, your two sons show me how
To shout and leap and jig at every chance,
To wave and jump and make this joyful row
And, even though I can't, to sing and dance.

HARMONICA

Her tunes were vamped through lipstick, played to show
The child I was just how to suck and blow
Enough to turn a tinny doh-re-mi
Into a broken-hearted melody,

The quaver in her stream of sopping notes
A dole queue in its Thirties overcoats
Whistling through nostalgias of gaslit
Chromatics proletarian with spit.

Her elbows planted on her bony knees
Moved up and down to breathy harmonies,
The busker in her picking up by ear
A smoke-filled, wheezy-chested atmosphere,

Her mothballed coat and man-sized walking boots
Shook with coughs and giggles, red-veined hoots,
The racket stopping so she could begin
Another tumblerful of Gordon's gin;

On every birthday calling to rehearse
A sixpence just discovered in her purse
Then drawing breath to cup each phrase between
Big chip-nailed hands orange with nicotine.

The cancer caught her quickly, left her grim,
The price, she said, for years of keeping slim;
A different world then, one that had no cure
For a life so unconventionally pure:

A game brunette, a card, as bold as brass,
Who dragged herself downstairs, turned on the gas,
And died between the lethal suck and blow
Of brick-vents in her basement studio.

THE MAGNIFYING GLASS

His fingers tied this thin red nylon string
I slowly disentangle from the box,
                Its cardboard flap
                    Bent inwards like a damaged wing
                          That, lifted, lightly shocks
His young face in its 1940s snap
Astonished at how fifty years could pass
Before his son went rummaging to find
Amongst these odds and ends he left behind
                    No magnifying glass.

A cribbage board with two loose pegs, a tin
Long emptied of its Meggezones, a book
                On graining wood
          Two rusty staples nestle in,
                    These dice his big hand shook
To show the way luck rolled in parenthood,
Each double six a smile inside a sigh
And, in the way that tenderness extends,
I see the face I ask the missing lens
                To raise and magnify.

Slipped down the sofa, hidden somewhere safe,
I need it now to unpick all these knots
              Minutely tied
                  As clove and reef and half-hitch chafe
                The edges of his box,
A past, a reassembled space to hide
This gift mislaid as soon as it was bought,
Its silver rim, its cool opthalmic weight
Reflecting love's bright power to concentrate
                    Or, pulled away, distort.

GREENSLEEVES

Blackberry, exhausted, still clutched to itself
Inside this engine with its snapped red fan,
Crashes in slow-motion out of undergrowth
Through the bonnet of a capsized ice-cream van,
Joins hose and perished rubber in the seal
Of an August's sun-crunched windscreen where, concussed,
Bindweed's cam-shafted cornets blow the grill
As dew kick-starts accelerating rust,
And where the bone-shook driver sat a rake
Of ivy leaves sharp frosts have brought up short
Lets autumn put its foot down on the brake
And bring the whole contraption to a halt.

SALIX CONTORTA

Grow little willow,
Twist into the wind,
Rave around the stem
Where your label is pinned,

Dance to its Latin,
Shake and fling the rain,
Reel with the robin
Round the ring in your grain,

Jitterbug with sunshine,
Go po-going through spring,
Leave sycamore and ash
To their own scattering,

Foxtrot over summer
With parsley and cowslip,
Hornpipe with the blackbirds'
Toodle-toodlepip,

And climb, twisted willow,
This trellised song alone
After I, who sang it,
Am nitrogen and bone.

SNOWDROPS

Each head is a blipped
white pulse of cold
swept intermittently
through a glacial January
to scatter in the grass
and its cratered verge of mud and ice
by an upended wheelie bin,
a frost-mantled green plastic recycling box.

We prize them exactly for this surprise,
for their armatures
and the chill they contain.
They help us survive
the tingling loss of motor skills
accumulating freezes bring
as stars on winter circuits get wired in;
gaps in transmission,
static in the fingertips,
sheaths peeled back from nerve ends in the dark,
a refrigerated intake of breath
with loss of all hope when the car won't start
and, padded and gloved for our half-hour hike,
the glance we exchange,
a complicated recognition
turning over, for a moment, the heart.

A CRYSTAL SKULL

Uplights strip down a mind
chill reassembles in
the brainwashed glass behind
her analgesic grin;
smashed embolisms, beads
of gas and shivered air,
opacity that seeds
a shattering idea.
Inside her case she gleams
as blown reflections pack
the dim thought-bubbled dreams
of a stoned insomniac.
She stares out as we float
through mirrors on the wall
where lucent neck and throat
turn into pedestal,
our crazed exhaustions caught,
refracted and seen through
by sockets fumed with salt
dried tears calcine into,
as shadow hangs on tight
to soluble glass skin
inspired by iris light
dissolving like aspirin
among the gritted teeth
her glacial jawbone held,
it's *Ah* of frozen breath
the chisel's blow expelled.

THE CRACK

Here at the end of the Cornish waves
Flocked gulls white-top like Arras graves
I look out at their smashed up day,
Black boots of rock, hamfists of spray,
Foamed hawthorn on the shattered path
Zigzagging down to its aftermath,
And realize how close I was
In the slip, on the lichen's rotting boss,
To very nearly smashing up
My life's one piece of great good luck,
And how, as winds howl through the crack,
Your tiny figure hauls me back,

As the tube of an autumn afternoon
Squeezes, blob by blob, its moon,
And dusk's blue tooth-glass swirls and jars
Its eyeful of syringeing stars,
And shorelights chase a haunted sea
Into this makeshift cemetery
Where far, far out, gold-ringed, six-stoned,
You plant, kneecapped, white ankleboned,
Your heel of moss, its vanished weight,
These gulls like graves commemorate.

SEA SONG

The sun glints like a butcher's steel
On the ironwork pier where gulls pinwheel
And dumped newspapers, breaking free
From their print's demotic energy,
Go chasing down the snatched-at coast
On the coat-tails of a bow-tied ghost,
Some dead bandleader waving still
His baton to the drowning hill,
While tides in salt-white ankle socks
Step daintily among the rocks
And on the beach a hot wind blows
Sand dried between a million toes.
A million things the sun adores.
Ten of them, my love, are yours.

TOURNIQUETS

The North Sea, oilskinned, under wraps,
Has staged these street-lamped afternoons,
Its wings, its sky's hydraulic flaps
Powered invisibly by moons
As dusk sparks up and slowly draws
Above the pubs and burger bars
To drop clean through the coast's glass floor
Its perforated packs of stars.

In shelters where they come to score
Their colonies of hoods and caps
Float on the oceanic roar
Inside a shingle bank's collapse,
Its snarled up lines, its drum of stones
That slow the sea's spin cycle, drown
The ringtones on their tin-eared phones
To pull the sky wordlessly down,

And still they shell out, still they think
He's brilliant as he strips them clean
Of store-tagged iPhones for a wink
And warm foil wraps of Ketamine;
And crooked, as Octobers craze
With smoke and soluble sunshine,
Blood spiders through rag tourniquets
In autumn's faintly tracked decline.

DOODLE

Its swims up like a tadpole, thin biro
That wriggles through the neon's coral light
And absentmindedly begins to grow
To blotchy half-life tentacled with white.
At this stage you're uncertain, wonder why
You're phoning her on such a weak excuse
As scribbled lines trail tangles of algae
That drift and intricately reproduce.
It's always when you're doing something else,
Your concentration, lowered in its cage,
Traps bubbles of attention as they burst,
Precipitates this inky haemorrhage
And leaves a tube fed aftermath, a caul
Of puffy membranes, brainwaves, EEG's,
A plunge into narcosis, its freefall
Through blue synapses, mock neurologies.
You push it, subarachnoid, blot by blot
Into the skull shaped pressure of your trance
And then hang up, surprised at what you've got,
Astonished at its insignificance;
And sometimes one is beautiful, at least
Mysterious and eye-catching enough
To tuck away unblemished and uncreased
With bills, receipts, old letters, photographs,
Until one day it flutters from the past
Pulled out between old envelopes to glide
And land with dog-eared postcards and her last
Hurt note to which you never quite replied.

LEMONADE

September with its blue monoxide plumes,
Its composts and its hospitable mists
Means shorter days and darker living rooms
And colours turning over like the twist
Of lemon in her glass of lemonade;
Sunk and tumoured, gnarled beyond repair
And trundled to a standstill someone's made
From a vanished summer's still untarnished air.

A crescent of fresh lipstick smears the rim,
A sip, the pink-caked fossil of a smile
That comes and goes each time she looks at him
Above the stream of bubbles' volatile,
Unhissed opacities and tiny sighs
The hollow glass distorts and amplifies.

A GLASS NECK

Electric floats, their zinc crates full of empties,
go rattling past the arc-lamped reservoir
as I crane out of the frosted third floor window
pushed open on monoxides and catarrh
and watch them stream along the shining asphalt,
blue, voltaic, caught out in the rain
that shatters on the iron roofs of the depot
showering bottletops and sodium
along this backlit street in South West London,
its nest of dripping wires, its orange cone.

One more wet morning ruffled by an absence
that hangs around and chills out on the chrome,
unearths its ghostly aluminium buggy
like space junk left dismantled on the moon.
Time hums and clicks, the mirror in the kitchen
floods over as the striplight flickers on
and drifts with dipping pot plants and fridge magnets
where, stepped into its pool of cold neon,
she blew, pink-skinned, across a rinsed milk bottle
and set its glass neck whooping like a swan.

SIGNAL FAILURE

Into this well of Camden submarine
with silver bottletops our luck has tossed
gold tins, black laddered tights, green Silly String
leapfrogging tracks and sleepers, bricked-up moss.
I smile at her. She blanks me. Ring-pulls gleam
metallic with the sour taste of a moon
that crashed here in the 60's, out of steam,
among stoved-in egg-boxes of high-rise,
their scaffolding still crating up a sky
milk floated winter mornings oxidize.

SILVER

It was the colour you got for coming second,
No. 2,
that significant, socially polished number;
all the best things came in twos,
binary codes, wings, ovaries,
anything more involved adjustment,
the psychological fuss of group dynamics,
anything less
an unconsoling loneliness.
She met him thirteen weeks ago
basking in the glazed, blue-dyed lagoon
of a rooftop office party,
and last weekend walked out on me.
As she is at pains to point out
I still have her affection, her respect;
all yesterday I loafed at home half-pissed
and ended on my hands and knees
red-necked and shaky-legged, a medalist.

AMMONITE

Blip by drizzling blip the scan
clarified this sonic ghost;
its crushed white gloves of calcium
and head of turned ultramarine
had left us feeling petrified,
giddy, uninvented.
Your cry that night
released a scented hush that haunts the room,
a sterile punch of panicked air
that raised the fading strap marks of your bra;
way back in the sinuses
our foetus bit its shrivelled fist
then slipped away
on saline,
grimly limelit bones,
migrations on the cold blue of the screen.
Its shapes would rematerialize
later in our unmade bed,
soft fossils in the chalk-white sheets
that wavered as you brushed them out,
brief casts, a laundered absence.
Passionately, transparently,
you rocked and cried yourself to sleep
curled beneath our naked bulb;
tears, salt-splintered filaments,
their whorls and urchin spines of light
embedded in the silence with
the painful, freakish coral of your tongue.

MUD IN HER EYE

"They drink her health, who stoops before she starts",
Whispered Jack, black Jack, to his spoiled Queen Of Hearts
As the King Of Diamonds carboniferously sighed
"They're gassing again, the blind widow's arrived"
And Luck shook its cap and pig's bladder to shout
Through the whole house of cards "You may think that you're out,
But the soul's moonlit ounces cannot be weighed
Nor the soot-blackened nails of the Queen Of Spades
Be prized from the dark once the Jokers are laid.
Face down she lies, the blue-bearded bride,
Untrumpeted, foxgloved, white-broomed in her ride,
With mud in her eye, weed binding her hair,
Red mercury rimming her kohl-lined stare
Raked up with the stars in their mill race again
Where time is the shivered waste product of pain".

A PRETTY KETTLE OF FISH

Punctured it was, dented, blackened by smoke,
forgotten on a yellow patch of grass.
Three trout were tipped in head first,
sharp tails dripping in the sun,
arched scales breathed on and dim.
Was this an oily rainbow's end,
a tear in the glistening fabric of things,
where unofficial lives break camp
leaving sunshine and drizzle,
prismatic damp?
Hurrying by at this rusty, Octoberish hour
a stranger might see
the breathlessly insignificant birth
of a disused cliché,
then rush down a towpath that follows a signpost
to a cloud of diesel
hung on a dangerous bend
furled in a silvery
fish-eye mirror
with red tail lights
and the vanishing bus
a tiny rain suspends.

DEVILSBIT

A fox leapt through the nitrates
That ate her orange dress
Scattering white spiders
Along a shivered wrist;
The Lady's Smock and Toadflax,
The Devilsbit for days
Astonished at the flashbulbs'
Brief forensic blaze
That split the twisted hornbeam
To let her soul escape
Its shawl of weeds through funneled dusk
And broken plastic tape:

A shaky hand-held camera,
The room's big-shadowed screen,
Arc lamps, Konica lenses,
Blue sheets of polythene
Around the dog filled coppice,
The unearthed skeleton
Confused with charms and fillings,
A gold ringed finger bone,
Black roots clumped with peroxide,
A struck kneecap, a skull,
The torn cobweb a frost threw up
She'd coughed and swallowed whole.

MATTHEW SMITH

His feel for her is too hard to resist.
This rose that blows along her right hand breast
And tugs its zigzag greenery has caught
A breath that fills and empties her chemise;
That crudely mimicked nipple almost rhymes
With the soft, lopsided purée of her lips,
And the inward gaze, the lead-lined lids,
Turn introspection outwards, as if thought
Were merely physiology. Her face,
Half-baked beneath a sheet of sunlit glass,
Is still as tender, still as resolute
As when she posed in that oppressive room
And his lymphatic palette thickened up
The oestrogen she pumped into the gloom.

His own self-portrait shows a moderate man,
A black coat with brass buttons and a hat,
A boiled and flat ironed shirtfront and a tie
Not too ornate, but lively; on his nose
Those pebble-lensed wire spectacles protect
A blank look from the even blanker stares
Beyond each wall. He won't give much away
Apart, of course, from *'feeling, science and praise,'*
And small gifts, like this necklace that she wears,
A fringe of catmint rounded into stones
Against the heated density of flesh
And the deeply buried secret of her bones.

PILLION

They zip, night-blind, down cats-eyed lanes
On chrome, white-walled coaxials,
Till moonlight in its high street chains,
Unvisored, icicles his smiles,

Then, finned and nacelled, nose coned, cowled,
He hits black ice, her starry ride
Ploughed under an Orion's wheels
As lamps, air-ambulanced, arrive:

Plugged in, tubed up, sky high on pills
She hangs on tight into her teens,
Bleep-bleeps to let them know speed kills
Dead slow on blue amphetamines.

BLACKSPOT

You leave the spine road tingling in darkness
and only come-to hours later
hung up in a tangle of birches
on the moon-bitten rim of the ditch.
So many bad things that happen
cannot be picked up or stretchered away,
must wait for a difficult daybreak,
another bone idle cold snap;
the weird jut of words forking out onto a white page,
the walking stick of a question mark,
bent twigs tapping the window,
arthritic, anxious to tell
whoever is willing to listen
their awkward suspicion
that the ice has cracked on the puddle,
that the splinter picked out by your smashed headlamp
has lodged in the daylight and started to thaw;
and for all you know you could still be there,
the engine forever ticking over,
the nearside front wheel spinning still
with only the migraine of flashing blue lights
and the hedge-baffled sirens coming and going
but failing to break the spell.

A SLIGHT DELAY

A graveyard likes a sunny day,
Especially in those corners where
The stones' preponderance of grey
Collects the monolithic air

And cockeyed headstones lend their weight
To epitaphs as autumns lean
Lengthways into the desolate
Corruptions of South London green.

At Denmark Hill the sun came out
And from the window of the train
October, like a tickled trout,
Resurfaced through a week of rain,

And vases straightened, granite shone,
A damp gleam tracked a plastic hose,
An angel hoicked a marble urn,
Its legs turned smoothly varicose;

Each plot filled with lopsided light
And meaning as we trundled past
Packed face to face and glad to get
Our journey underway at last.

A SHORT HISTORY OF MORNINGS

Thirteen main types, all easily classifiable,
all, so far, resisted. A few break through though;
the queasy mist around a dog-rose,
the optical clarity of an early June dawn,
the zinc tank of November, the knocking of its drowned.
They form a sort of delivery system, bucket and claw
on a moss-disfigured conveyor belt trundling always towards
whatever light is available wherever we happen to be.
Take this October Sunday for instance. Wake with headache,
Tiptoe through the rewired insularities of dawn,
swallow three pills of utter, arctic whiteness
and drink from a glass that becomes itself the purest meltwater
at one with the hum of the freezer and the magnets dotting the
fridge.

As in any history there has to be a last one
(unless there is a resurrection or a revised edition)
when, alone or in company, knowingly or unknowingly,
you attend at a valedictory sampling
the taken-for-granted freshly washed, the sparkling.
When you wake and ask yourself "Was I there last night?"
Or, unfathomably, "Was it me? Was it me?"
And all you hear is the wind
and the lamps click off down the empty road
and all of the autumn leaves scratching, scratching away
in the bitterly impecunious sepia
of the obscure, the unfinished, the soon-to-be-completed,
the blackbird and thrush haunted, almost light-hearted,
spiked obituary.

TIPPEX

It goes on like emulsion, dulls and dries
To shit-frilled twigs a winter calcifies,
Stiff brushwork, plastered jottings, buds and clots
Of clay-piped semi-colons, stucco'd dots;

As words cling to obliterated fact
Masked typefaces shine briefly and impact,
A fluent whiteout, cultured impasto,
Faint meanings on brisk pedestals of snow,

Precarious, intensified, somehow
Much closer to the porous here and now.
Before I used this stuff my botched first drafts,
Blue-biro'd leaves and faulty holographs,

Were stashed in carboned piles beneath the sweet
Creamed evolutions of the finished sheet.
Now all those crabbed syllabics I repressed
Are casts inside this brittle palimpsest,

A caulked one-off, a thickly meerschaumed text
That trapped me in the chalk of what came next
Where fossilizing rhyme broke up and sank
And left the sedimentary future blank.

AN IDLE BASK

Amongst upended bottles and cracked jars
        Piled in their plastic box
                This strange frog grew,
A bulb of mud that pulsed and shocked
        Through green and cloudy glass
        As light and shadow passed
Or moths spun in the headlamps of our cars
        And time, peered into, flew,

While autumn leaves swirled round and fell like days
        We never really used
                But pushed aside;
A beauty all the trees refused
        Turned brittle, scraped and brushed
        With last September's dust
Then raked and shovelled up to feed the blaze
        That billowed, roared and died.

Through all these fires the frog declined to jump.
        I'd got so used to it
                I'd even prized
Its stillness as a kind of wit,
        Its muddiness as grace,
        Its grip on time and place
Exerted by a chilly rubber stump
        Late sunshine galvanized.

Last night it was so difficult to spot
        I knew that it was lost;
                Old secrets rot,
An idle bask the sun embossed
        Had hopped and from its mark
        Dropped sheer into the dark
With all those things half-loved but done without
        Then, dried and smudged, forgot.

From

The Nick of Time

Shoestring Press

2014

THE ICE HOUSE

A touch of Brunelleschi in its dome
        Glimpsed through the trees
Intrigued us just enough to cross the stream
And enter, through its map of yellow moss,
A culture that pre-dated CFCs
And died out with the big house years ago
To leave this lichened symbol of its loss
Washed over by new money's undertow.

It's trashed now, full of rubble, silver tins,
        Chunked styrofoam
And puddles growing ice like second skins
As we climb down a hundred years too late
To shiver underneath its brick-lined dome
Not daring to turn round or test the floor
And shocked at how the rich can insulate
Their world against the cold hands of the poor.

Each step is a cut passage through the years
        To rush us past
Lost generations, glacial chandeliers,
Their drops of sunlight dangling in the rain
As slow meltwater, loosening at last,
Wells up through alder, ash and sycamore
And leaves such breathless ghosts of ice to drain
Down through the rubbish piled against the door.

Go down once more, go back into the dark,
        And hack into
The frozen heart of money's landscaped park,
Exhume old light, release its bubbled air
And feel your lips and fingers turning blue
Then cart it back and watch exhaustion pass
In candlelight through crystal as you stare
At all your labour chiming in a glass.

THE HOLLY LEAF

For months she'd watched its glossy green
Begin to mottle, blotch and fade
Then thin to rigging winds picked clean,
Warm breezes fussily crocheted,
Snagged on a shrub, hung out to dry
Cat's-cradled by a cobweb, blown
From inside out to calcify
On weed-cracked crazy paving stone,
Until, snared by white plastering,
Still trying to give earth the slip,
With yellow gloves it entered spring
Between her thumb and fingertip.

She'd left it on the kitchen sill
To bleach with J cloths in the sun,
Watched autumn gauzily unveil,
Headlamps strip search its skeleton;
A peek into an afterlife
As beauty, ceasing to exist,
Still goes on looking for itself,
Becomes its own anatomist,
Lays bare the damage, lets her heart
Respond again to what love asks
Between electrodes that jump start
Its journey back through tube and mask

Then leaves her drifting in the ward,
The night light like a cold blue star
Above her silver bed's clipboard,
Its graphs, its felt-tipped DNR.
We cleaned and hoovered, placed the leaf
Reflectively on stainless steel,
A gift, a charm against our grief
To catch her spirit by the heel

As, moving round an empty house,
It tries each closed glass panelled door
And, weightless in the polished hush,
Slips through them like a conjuror.

SEXING SKELETONS

The long bones and the pelvis are our clues
Now flesh is an abstraction, now the skin,
The coloured eye, the philtrum, lips and nose
Shrink back to leave just teeth stuck in the grin.

We mix-and-match them, pair them up to find
Who goes with who in this new afterlife,
And so long dead they surely will not mind;
We sort the bones for husband, bones for wife,

Their skulls, their jaws dropped open for old wine
Or maggots in dead tongues that wagged to prize
The sexiness of talus, sternum, spine
Time strips and agricultures pulverize.

We catalogue them, lay them side by side,
The disarticulated made to stir,
To find, deep in their carbon, ossified,
This bias for the male we disinter.

So even dead some women, second best,
Are dug up, disassembled, reassigned
And rattled by each wrong, bone-headed guess
Amongst the ribs and hips they leave behind.

Our x-rays catch them as they incandesce,
Stripped bare, irradiated, cheated twice,
Now light years from the rags of their last dress
And held up to the lamp in sacrifice.

WATER BOATMAN

A connoisseur of cooling surface tension
And all the polished ways a cloudscape flows,
He stops and brings your senses to attention,
Then tenses, walks away on glass tiptoes,

Or hangs and, upside down, collects a bubble,
Descending in its silvery membrane,
To plumb the depths and, like a spirit level,
Bob up into stability again.

When autumn and refraction make days shorter
He gathers dusk around him like a shawl
Then tips a battered moon into the water
To prove the garden pond unspillable.

He snatches your miraculous affection
With ways to sink or swim and lets you choose
To step out under stars from your reflection
And walk on water wearing his glass shoes.

PAPERWEIGHT

A cold spring sunshine comes and goes
Sliced up by our Venetian blind
And in between it briefly snows.
We stare out of our window thrilled
With each delicious change of mind
And buoyant, airtight, vacuum sealed.

So this is what it's like to be
A toy in someone else's life
With moving parts that think they're free,
Or faces pressed to blobs of glue,
An underwater man and wife
Looked down upon and deep into.

Who tips us up? Inverts our room
And snows us with these whites and golds
As aqueously we assume,
Suspended in the morning's glare,
That something like a future holds
Our endlessly recycled stare?

Our dreams are tidal and their sky
Sucked back into sleep's hinterland
Blows inside out to amplify
This silence that a touch might break.
A high wind with its blue glass hand
Turns up to give us one more shake.

IMPERIAL LEATHER

Although he's gone
She still can't wash her hands of him,
Can't miss the wet reflection in each tile
Or how he shone
Through steam that made the glass shelves swim
With cracked ceramic glimpses of his smile
And can't explain
Why, labelless, his cherished slip of soap
Still yellows on the porcelain
Decaying like some ghostly isotope.

He's there today
And as she dips one blue-veined wrist
And gathers lather in each wrinkled hand
Light starts to play
Inside his mirror's fume of mist
She's delicately come to understand:
She runs both taps
And hums and gently turns her thinning ring
And rinses it and thinks, perhaps,
"His slip of soap is slowly vanishing,

What will I do
When this, the very last of him,
Dissolves and leaves me finally alone?
Diminish too?
Stand sideways in the light and thin
To finely brushed and powdered skin and bone?"
The radio
Playing Bach and Schubert now till late
Is drowned out by the water's flow
As note by note the songs disintegrate.

        Nothing will last
   But while it does she watches him
Above the silver plug chain in the sink.
        Her past is past,
    His life a tidemark round the rim
And love an old skin slowly turning pink.
         She'll lose him soon,
Look up one night into a frosted pane
    On which a paring of the moon
Will break and wash away in summer rain.

GLACIER MINTS

        A morbid immobility
Turned her into the sort of geographical feature
            Sheet ice transmutes,
A glass terrain we all tip-toed around;
        Her chair an intricate dead tree
            And, clutched like roots,
        Her gnarled hands sprouting frigidly,
            Her lap a polar mound
Of misty wrappers smoothed out, sticky-backed,
That glistened like some blue-eyed cataract.

        You entered through a scent of mint
And found yourself in a different weather system,
            Breath visible
On cut glass in her gleaming living room
        And carrying an arctic hint,
            Confected chill
        That washed her like an aquatint,
            A frosted bloom
Suffusing every kidney spot and crease
Reflected in the mirrored mantlepiece.

        On Sunday nights the TV was outstared
With tear ducts slowly leaking their glacial debris,
            Her brittle jaw
Set firm as splintered sugar turned opaque
        Surviving under snow-white hair
            The muffled roar
        As bergs of memory calved and sheared
            And in their wake
Light ricocheted through frost to sting her eyes
And all our stone cold faces crystallized.

BEATRICE CENCI
Guido Reni 17th C
Original in Rome

      She hung around our scullery,
Looked down on us from its damp plastered wall
And "wasn't bad for fifteen bob" he said.
      She peered out into shade
Serenely waiting for sunlight to fall
With all the eerie patience of the dead
      Who, picked up for a song,
      Are sure it won't be long,
The afterlife has simply been delayed.

      She smiles, looks over her shoulder
And murky now with olives, browns and creams
Stares out into an emptiness nonplussed
      Through varnishes that crack
On tin-tacked canvas splitting at the seams,
Still shaping up to slip past lamplit dust,
      Escape her time and name
      And shimmy from the frame,
Shake off loose flakes, step out and not look back.

      Maybe that's why he picked her up
In Angel's junk shop eighty years ago
Appealing as she must have to his sense
      Of beauty and fair play
With eyes that saw what he would never know
Through almond lids and puddled innocence,
      Attentiveness just missed
      By this late copyist,
A neck the clumsy brushstrokes still betray.

    I've tucked her underneath my arm
In bubblewrap to insulate her spell,
Secured her with two bows of garden string
    To bring her safely home
And if I could I'd bring him back as well
To play the holy fool again, to sing
    And like some dusty saint
    Release her from her paint
And dance behind her all the way to Rome.

OBSEQUIES

She hovers by an angel white as chalk
Then kneels in her red coat to tend his grave
And while she digs she shuts her eyes to talk
As though to an old man who's misbehaved.
I stare out of the window, cannot hear
This dressing down of some poor skeleton,
But what she says seems passionate, sincere,
While I, deaf like the dead, stand looking on
At all these mossed inscriptions that retrace
The stone stabilities of time and place,
Remembering grey ashes poured from urns,
My father first, then mother, always late,
Their view a field of stars that slowly turns,
Their graves eternally approximate.

I envy her carved headstone and its power,
Her faithfulness on this bright Easter day,
A sense that someone dead can yet somehow
Become, sneaked in by love, a stowaway;
Curl up in scent still haunting an old scarf,
Slip in between a first and second glance,
Duck down behind themselves in photographs,
Leave body heat where clouds of midges dance.
Elusive, solemn, shy, mischievious,
What's left of them goes living on in us,
And so today I'm glad that nothing much
Will pierce this mix of sunshine and exhaust
Or their everlasting silence that's a touch
Indignant now at what the coffins cost.

TRIANGLE

      A whitewashed wall
And wooden ladder painted black
        Made up the triangle
Of cables, masts and rigging, harbour views
All framed by its sun-struck hypotenuse
        Left angled to
Its 45 degrees of white and blue
From which, it seems, there was no turning back.

        She took a breath
Then with crossed fingers closed her eyes
        To blindly dodge beneath
And something in the taut way that she went
Seemed tentatively held to circumvent
        Her fear, its weight
That made her orange T-shirt hesitate
And red, stuck in its spectrum, agonize.

        When she emerged
Relief swept through her like a gale
        As ancient sunlight surged
And shadow, like a skeleton that stole
Her beauty from inside the bone-white wall,
        Somehow jumped clean
Out of its small three-sided world to mean
That everything that day would turn out well.

STYLUS

A thrush's piped song
gets stuck on a thorn
that picks out its whistle
lead-lined with moonlight
heart-piercingly caught
on ivy climbed through the hole in the wall,
where, a snail-track ago,
a fox with a fire in its tail slunk through,
and where now
dusks wells to fulfilment
round an oil lamp and a smoky hollyhock.
Who could have known
that our spat in the sun
with its loose threads of rain,
its raffia jacketed bottle of wine
on a sleeveless day propped at an easel would come
to such an astonished unravelling?
Drainings like this
run too quick and too deep for the colourist;
for violet to be indelibly fixed
or gentian never acrylicly stilled
is the failure of water, its spring loaded brush:
or the night prove us wrong
with its hisses and scratches, our thin tempered needle
that picks up the silver fox fur and the torn chickenwire,
balanced and scored on their fineness, a theme
in the thrush's occluded song.

FLOC

I am the dog of Michel Gallimard
who 54 years ago disappeared
returning to tell you of how the soul flew
from the broken-necked body of Albert Camus
head first from his seat to the back of the car
past the wife and the daughter of poor Gallimard
who, thrown in the air, both leapt for his soul
as he would have once at the mouth of his goal,
but came down hands empty beside the two men
trapped in the Vega and dying in Sens.
All lay there and waited not knowing I knew
that the doctor arriving was Marcel Camus,
too late for Albert but possessing the same
strange, Sisyphian, Gallic surname.
Dazed they got up and staggered while I,
sniffing a mystery, unable to die,
limped off to worry, to puzzle, perplex
obsessives inventing the things that came next
under the plane trees, the plane trees of Sens
as the air turned to liquid, the liquid to bronze,
while high overhead in the silence a bird
was repeatedly trilling *absurd, absurd*.
I've run with this now for so many years
through distortions of language and cameras and tears
but when I lit out the whole thing was a whim
as ghostly and insubstantial as film,
and, yes, like a movie, a movie that starred
the vanishing dog of Michel Gallimard.

UNDERSTUDY

Time, the scene-shifter, has done it again,
This sink and this mirror weren't here before,
Nor this old razor blade spotlit to explain
Her grubby white towel's arterial spoor,
As love, the scene-stealer, swans in from the wings,
Shaking a blisterpack, making a fist
Through a snowstorm of tissues pain numbingly flings
And wearing, like bangles, red cuts round her wrist.

The actor who played me is off, indisposed,
So, under-rehearsed, blood smeared on my hand,
I'm shoved on in a play I wrongly supposed
A light-hearted romance the critics had panned,
Waiting in rain for the fourth wall to break
With ambulance men at their curtain-calls
And the cock-eyed bow she's managed to take
And the hiss of wet tyres fading out like applause.

THE AFTERLIVES OF THE ANARCHISTS

Those staples in their foursquare silver strips
        Stacked upward like some brutalist
                Manhatten office block
           Were teased apart by fingertips
And, jammed down in the stapler at half-cock,
         Sent shockwaves up my wrist
               Then pushed back in
                  They pierced the skin,
          Refusing to align
With folded A4's creased and crooked spine.

Another bead of blood. Another botch.
        Another pamphlet not quite straight
            To join the dodgy pile,
       Another squat for Special Branch to watch.
In those days no emoticons would smile,
          No app would re-collate
              The author's rage
               At each slipped page
           As blood and bits of skin
Smeared Proudhon, Stirner, Goldman, Bakunin.

Still edgy and implacable they've gone
        With smudges, thumbprints, films of dust,
            Blurred ghosts that, hand-cranked, roll
     From cyclostyle to silicon
Through purple aniline and methanol
         As digital exhaust
             Shows they survive
             In some hard drive
          And, scanned, downloaded, binned,
Shrug off the world their staples underpinned.

A DIFFERENCE OF OPINION

We can only imagine what a man thinks
When he's just lost his head on the guillotine
From the twenty or so of Lavoisier's blinks
And the thoughts, if any, he had in between;

A chance, as I feel the edge of her tongue
Sharp and ill-tempered, go whispering by,
To blink from the basket and, bloodily swung,
Signal at last that we see eye to eye.

BLUEBELL

Timing let you down
and spring's aggressive candour
pushed you on,
your daredevil blue
testing the air
in a misty, leaf-cut
sunbeam's flare.
Your rush to be a botanical star,
crushed by a frost, proved premature,
a two day singularity
that wasn't the frailest, the bluest, the first
April has shrunk to slake its thirst.

Later, with the smoky blue they prized,
the mushroom haunted woods were colonized
and mornings were a picnic for the thousands that came after
composing their cushions and pillows for summer,
for children lost in the breath-ghosted air
and the mists drinking their laughter.

RADIUM

Girls on the nightshift, a luminous pose,
Their brushes of Undark licked to a point,
Glow through this negative, over-exposed
As nitrates turn their beauty back-to-front;
Their gestures and reversals are obscure,
Dim body counts, incinerating light,
Translucent features, laughter's spooky burr
Sunk into darkness, flaring inside-out.

It's too late now to catch the way things went,
Uranium has filleted the air,
Fluorescent jaws lit up with what was meant,
Lips turned candescent, tongues gone nuclear;
Absorbed in dials and minute hands they trace
With brushstrokes what their radiance destroyed
As, freaked with paint, the grins that gut each face,
Outshining bones, burn through the celluloid.

GLASS CEILING

Skittering over wet gravel
ionized glints undermined
the moon on a high water table
dissolvingly silver-lined
black ice crazing on puddles
splintering under court shoes,
diffusing the steps she had taken
on the way she determined to lose.

Stealing through clinical darkness
not even the stars dispelled
she came in a wobble of torchlight
to banks where mud craters held
fragments of chalk like those tablets
she'd glassily hoarded to keep
for her short-sighted walk into water,
her broken appointment with sleep.

Trailing a necklace of bubbles,
as chilled out as she'd ever been,
she gazed at the water's glass ceiling
through algae and torn polythene
in weeds she'd pulled on turning over
with their hemlines of midges and flies
tidied and fussed by the river
and dressed for a stranger's eyes.

CHEERS

Here's to the tide and the moon it's outworn
And here's to your jawline halfway through a yawn
And here's to the anglepoised North Norfolk coast
Keeping its flocked oystercatchers engrossed,

And here's to fresh Easterlies siphoning sand
From dunes hourglass weather has sifted and panned
For shells and sharp shingle across the sea floor
Our shadows move gingerly down to explore,

Bobbing about, playing tag with a sun
As it wrinkles the beach leaving mud underdone,
Or spilling, when cloud cover threatens their spree,
In soft corrugations between you and me,

And here's to their feathering, ruffled inside
Edgy white waves on the tip-tilted tide
That sip at cold ankles, tickle with salts
Your drinkable heelcups a morning exalts.

From

A Song About You

Shoestring Press

2017

LUNULA

Wind turbines taper down at dusk to spear
a moon above the vertical sea wall,
pick up a breeze to idly manicure
with buds of cloud its brilliant cuticle,
clipped out by winter, pared by carbon blades,
and showcased as the Plough sparks up and flints,
its flashy Iron Age opulence downplayed
by algae gargling foam in my footprints.

All swallowed now, like me, as tides withdraw,
by darkness dragging waves that phosphoresce
around a figure lights have washed ashore
barelegged and stealing off in your blue dress,
footloose inside the shimmer of its cling
to perfume where your body once adhered
then, atomised with mist, diminishing
until, like grief, it almost disappears,
and numbed I feel these combers rake the sand
for crab and starfish, claw and empty shell
while at my back the ringed bone of your hand
scrapes down me with this icy fingernail.

TROMBICULA

Inching along as if each verb were mined
This rutilant bug moved over the page
Following blindly what sunlight divined,
A scarlet full-stop on a pilgrimage,
Altering meaning, infusing what's meant
With the cardinal truth of a penitent

Crawling toward what ink might reveal
As, clumsily trying to brush it away,
I leave just this smudge of rich cochineal,
Its crimson exhaust of smeared DNA
Streaked out to the blue-lined edge of A5
Where silences yellow, shadows arrive,

Filling with autumn my song about you,
The cost of that brittle red smile you wore
In the Pay & Display where, hectic, you flew
Through blotchy gold leaves to the clinic's glass door
While, fishing for silver, I poured out the price
Palm up in the rain like a sacrifice.

THE AGE OF STEAM

This was the line that took me for a walk
Through rain and forked lightning, chimneys of cloud,
Clinker, cow parsley, hardbitten chalk
Sleeper by sleeper the cutting devoured

When a hare sprung out from a clump of oxeyes
Zigzagging nozzles of lopped hollyhocks,
Hot-footing on cinders to galvanize
His lime-white bobtail through scalded snowdrops.

The old bunker saved him, bursts of fireweed
Heaving cracked tarmac where coal tenders stopped
Under gas mantles as, picking up speed,
He shot through a hedge and got his ears boxed.

The owl like a pilot light in its hornbeam
Burned sootily on, unblinking, quartz-eyed,
Giving a hoot for the lost age of steam
And the moon and the hare electrified.

SILVER MIST

Her ruined hull sinks into grass and sand
Or seems, as he draws near, to crest a dune,
Reminding him of something they once planned
                But didn't risk
                That wind-scoured afternoon
When spring rain lashed the war memorial,
Mossed letters on a white stone obelisk
                Where, facing the North Sea
                Their chill freemasonry
Stood shining to attention through each squall.

He tips the dusty jar up with a shake
Then, trudging round the carcass of this boat,
Sidestepping ashes scattered in her wake,
                He gives the lid a twist
                And, brushing down his coat,
Reads in the cursive stencil on her prow,
Sun-faded and alluring, *Silver Mist*,
                Italic strokes that host
                A calligraphic ghost
Still clinging to the sunlit here and now,

Still haunted by the dream that one more tide
Drawn by a moon will take her out to sea
And, cast off from her past, her leeward side,
                Fill her white sail
                With dusk's South Westerly,
Cold wave on wave collapsing to expose
Beyond their reach the still incalculable,
                A sense that what we mean
                Dissolved in iodine
Throws shadows on the new build bungalows,

While chiselled names are honoured and released,
Half-cut in lamplight, free as wind to sing
Through sand and grass their sentries once policed,
                Convinced that she,
                Buoyed up for one last fling
With tins and bottletops the tide outleans,
Is never really finished with the sea
                Lit by, through her beached years,
                Stars' icy chandeliers
She'll swing into and smash to smithereens.

WOMAN IN BLUE

Swung loose to drop a dress
My small gold-ringed left hand
That once made you tumesce
Has left me now unmanned,
Is fused into my spine
Where sharply drawn up knees
Stretch tendons, realign
A quarrel's symmetries.

Your analytic gaze
Triangulates my thighs,
Finds creases to erase,
Soft spots to atomise;
My belly, breast and face
Dismantled to placate
The temper you displace
With rectangles of paint,

Cross-sectioning an arm,
Manhandling hips into
This parallelogram
Of volumetric blue
Where right-angles reveal
Impastoed, dried and cracked,
My torso's triangle
Exactly inexact.

From roots in my red hair
To chilblains on each toe
Through pulled-on underwear
The pins and needles flow.
Slipped back into worn shoes,
Stone cold from my debut,
I find, beneath this bruise,
A bone to pick with you.

FISHEYE

Wind pulls out the gather
in the fish shop's nets of rain
on glass where bits of clingfilm
peel back to shrunk membrane
smeared with cabled lightbulbs
looped down the promenade,
B & Bs, guest houses,
white-stucco'd, crowned and starred,
shone bright enough to turn him
to a loser who, outcast,
stares back into his future
through the blurred lens of a past.

He lights out for his hostel
but hoodwinked by the blaze
of an arcade's incandescence
showered down on alleyways,
winds up inside this mirror
with its torsion of surprise
that twists, sucks in and swallows
lost shillings, chrome-rimmed eyes;
mercurial, time bulges
in his bright metallic grin
where the boy clean out of silver
slips through its tarnishing.

ON THE POSSIBILTY OF RECYCLING GOLD FROM THE MOUTHS OF THE DEAD

Submitted as a Phd thesis to the University of Breslau by Victor Scholz in 1940

Did they call for a viva voce,
The dead in their ash-smeared gowns,
When you talked through a golden future
Bought with a mouthful of crowns?

Did they, Dr Scholz, never thank you,
Those dead with their mouths open wide,
For treasuring them who were worthless,
For the bullion their smiles failed to hide?

Or imagine you silver haired, Victor,
On your uppers, clean out of loot,
Keeping schtum in the aftermath
With a cap and a black market suit,

Still nursing the sewn leather copy,
Blind stamped and hand tooled with a leaf
That thins out and flakes as your gold name escapes
From the past by the skin of its teeth?

DEAD MAN'S FINGERS

She sees him in the way his ink caps poke
through toils of spiteful blackberry and fire,
in Leylandii, in epiphanic smoke
and red hot pokers brandished to inspire
what light there is to purple, heat and glow,
to blind the bearded iris with its bulb,
smash lily-of-the-valley up to snow
through bluish April's desolate dissolve;

and now, beyond the ha-ha, tears are shed
for time his dead man's fingers might repair,
for rose and jonquil squandering spilt red,
for broken terracotta, web-strung air,
for dowdy moths white candles singed and burned
before her moistened thumb had snuffed their wicks
to smoke out love, to find, not love returned,
but, smudged with ash, still up to its old tricks.

A CARDBOARD WITCH

Last night I came across your cardboard witch
Abandoned in a box of playschool stuff,
Gold stars, crêpe paper boxes, dried felt tips
Forlorn and long forgotten in the loft

Along with greetings cards that all contained
Blue biro'd kisses heaped against a time
When glitter still shook out its ill-starred rain
And luck was silver horseshoes, love a rhyme.

Now luck is straws, pipe cleaners, peeling dots,
Stiff cartridge paper dusty years unscroll,
Fluffed Sellotape that sprouts and chimneypots
The hollow tube from unfurled kitchen roll

And all our charms and wishes have come home
Still clinging to what memory forsakes,
Surviving in dried glue and Styrofoam
The muffled crack each old adhesion makes,

Or perishing with pink elastic bands
That snap and ping, fly off into pitch dark
As, drawn on foolscap, blind to where they land,
Her crayoned face peers through the watermark.

WITCH HAZEL

I watch a towerblocked afternoon
haze out at dusk to skylined miles
of suburbs while a caustic moon
eats into polystyrene tiles,
bobs up beyond her rubber plant,
her calendar, its circled dates,
glass mist from her deodorant
a red street lamp irradiates
along with tubes of shower gell
as pee sparkles into the bowl,
a soluble glass wand, a spell
of aspirin and alcohol.
I turn and, pushing downwards, click
the childproof cap off, half expect
some liquid ghost to help her sleek
blue scalp squeeze from its screw-top neck
where wide-eyed, with a shouldered wince,
she towels her creased, unstoppered breast
then slips out of her talc footprints
and leaves the bathroom dispossessed.

COLD SHOULDER

I wake half-stoned, peer out to find
dawn unarrived, the night's dark grind

wheeled overhead now, dropping stars
into three huge blue reservoirs,

where, washed and filtered, astral grist,
they hang in cabinets of mist.

She stirs, throws back our bunched duvet,
one shoulder bared as fingers play

with eiderdown plucked at to dress
her goose-bumped, spine-chilled nakedness

while headlamps freeze her small pink heel,
ambush the room with light, reveal

what she, asleep, wants me to know,
things shadows fleeing shadows throw

onto, slashed by our thin strip-blind,
the white sheet of her made-up mind.

ESCAPOLOGY

Her barker, who gathers the drinkers in,
        Is small yet somehow
        Exudes a power
With his cave of a chest, his thick-lipped grin,
        Shouting the odds outside a pub
Where we, the latecomers, drift by to see
        A girl slipped from an anorak
        Weighed down with chains inside a sack
Then tied with rope, run through with swords,
        To turn and wriggle like a grub
        Blindly thrashing to set us free
From the spell of his fake atrocity.

She struggles while he takes the bucket round
        Then grunts to make
        Her grand escape
And, shimmied out of hessian, astounds.
        Her knee is grazed, her wrist contused,
Dust swells her tear ducts, jute inflames her eyes,
        But, bowed to blow a thankyou kiss
        From sacking's cast-off chrysallis,
She smiles and waves to make her damaged way
        Past city drinkers, carrying her shoes
        In search of ointments that disguise
The cuts and bruises love will cauterize.

We turn away, look down into our drink,
        Not sure or keen
        On what we've seen,
Feel conned by something we assumed extinct,
        Its stained tarpaulin, rope and chains,
        The leather bags in which he packs such things;
        And even her escape won't free
        Us from our own complicity
Or him, amongst his torture chamber props,
        From money and its grubby fling

   As, divied up before it rains,
He counts out what we've paid her for her pains.

I'd seen this as a child, this cameo,
      A frantic man
       With swords and chain
Explaining what the sack would undergo
    On the cobblestones of Tower Hill
With a voice at once both gravelled and depraved.
    His blades, unsheathed, were flashed and kissed
    Then swung in a red-knuckled fist
To pierce a trussed-up body's muffled cries,
    And blood, that wasn't meant to spill,
    Made sure this evening as she waved
Not one of us would walk away unscathed.

SCOOTER

As stone and granite start to cool
And, sensing that there's rain to come,
Lamps flicker on, diffuse and pool
Their orange drops of sodium,

She thrusts, bare-legged, towards the yew,
Kick-starts her ticklish journey back,
Outpaces dusk's slow-burn curfew
In trainers and blown anorak.

She flies through crazed, unweeded graves,
Zigzags towards gold thistled gates
Where ragstone hazardously paves
A nettled square that radiates

Footpaths she rattles down to scuff
Past angels, doves, an ivied wing,
Their weather-beaten griefs enough
To blur love's marble lettering;

Plays kiss chase with the dead again,
Their whiskered ferns, their overgrown
And lipless brush of moss sponged pain
Still stinging her grazed anklebone.

A PAIR OF BOOTS

I found a pair of steel-capped boots
My father lent me eight years back
"For a week or two, till the snow melts"
"And the thin ice", I murmured, "cracks".
They were too large, spring ice turned black
And years flew past snowdrift by drift.
"You can keep them now he's gone", Mum said,
Tongue-tied, tight-laced, a funeral gift.

I wore them once, for love, for duty,
Struck sparks and banged around until,
Not big enough to fill them properly,
I turned to what I could fulfill
And gave them to the Hospice shop
Where, brushed up like a spruced heirloom,
With a Gift Aid code and a £5 tag
They stood guard by the changing room.

I peered in past an angled window,
Its chrome-braced shelves of bric-a-brac,
And in each flared, sun-thrown reflection
My grin brought his grin briefly back
As, dustily, I glimpsed my father
Slipped toe-tagged from his stainless drawer,
Marched barefoot from his funeral parlour,
Come for his boots through the swung glass door.

YES

No one is right all of the time
so I listen
in this loft by the sea
to shifts of pitch and tone
in the message you left for me
drowned out by atmospherics,
a gobbledegook of blips
and oceanic streamings
as I plunge into static and fish
through transatlantic distortions
for the sibilant tail of a *'yes'*.

Truth today takes up less space,
slimline on tablets,
sunk with transponders,
miniaturized in pings and tweets,
but here, now, I have it to hand
in a still locatable you.
Who cares that nothing is going as planned
if one good word gets through?

New Poems

THE WHITE SPARROW

Towards the end and sightless
she woke up to swear
she'd seen a white sparrow
shaking off drops of rain
under the photinia.
Tonight, clearing our garden,
I glimpse the crestfallen ghost
of a robin,
its red breast drained
to a white affront,
its stillness lit
by the first spill of dusk,
adding a touch of make-believe
to forked-up roots,
the hole they leave;
a delicate beat
as though warmth still clings
to the thin white bands
of slipped-off rings:
impossibilities
and their possible wings.

HINDSIGHT

                Spring sun comes splashing through
Stained glass to rinse and throw washed colours up the wall,
           Dispels, unwished, dissoluble,
     One more cold morning waking without you,

             Where mirage is more real
Than blobs of lead and solder holding blemished panes
            An April flushes out in stains
    To charm from dullness what its depths conceal,

              Or so I think as red
Saturates our pillows and, radiating, dyes
            White sheets that burn to carbonize
      My brittle shadow charcoaled on our bed.

             Hindsight or *deja vu*?
Blindsided by our room's incinerating dust
           I watch you looking back nonplussed
    At all the small white lies you now see through,

             Transparent in your mime
To turn up in the mirror you swore it dropped behind
             That earring we could never find
    And show me how it lay there all the time.

TOMFOOLERY

I found a gift-tag tailed with silver string
dropped by our bed, ironically heart-shaped,
gold cardboard, unattached to anything,
attracting bits of fluff and Sellotape
and, placed between your hairbrush and your pills
with ribbon from the final gift you wrapped,
reflected in a mirror that revealed
With all my love blue-biro'd on the back.

Your present, a belated *jeu d'esprit*,
this black and orange clip-on kipper tie,
its flourish of your old tomfoolery
intended to, with love, mock-horrify,
turned up too late to carry off the joke
but left me grateful, knowing how you'd tried,
still hearing laughter, stifled as I woke,
and truly, by the morning, horrified.

AT FIRST I FAILED

At first I failed, made light of their escape
As chasing leaves became a letting go
And summer, blown through hedges, lost its shape,

While brooms, that once kept both out lives shipshape,
Abandoned in long grass too wet to mow,
Let handfuls, in their panoply, escape,

And left me, cold at dusk, to bow and scrape,
Until winds dropped and, snatched at on tiptoe,
They hung where a new brittleness took shape

Or swept around me, flourished like a cape
Shook out with moths and stars as, shocked, a crow
Soared into darkness, cawed at their escape.

They floated down like ruined ticker tape
That filled the air with news of you to show,
Lit by the bonfire, how your hectic shape,

Chased stick-like through its flicker book landscape
By brush and rake, by broken-handled hoe,
Had made, curled up, consumed and changing shape,
At last, in smoke and ashes, its escape.

LIFEBUOY
for Daisy Dennis

When asked the secret of her skin and hair
        She'd gathered up her scattered wits
And, beaming from her sunlit wicker chair,
            Offered like a gift,
New dentures slipping, one wry quip *"Lifebuoy"*;
Remembering the times she soaped me down
Naked on her oak-leafed tabletop,
        Her blue rimmed bowl, its cool alloy
Smooth beneath my feet, her steady frown
                My earliest devotion,
A laying on of palms to wash away
Astringently the dirt from each scoured day.

I was the only child she never had,
        Brought to her when lost tempers snapped
And, while the world went briefly mad,
           Dropped helpless in her lap,
Consoled with water, flannelled with *Lifebuoy*
Then rinsed, towelled dry and dusted off with talc,
Its scented clouds of powder we inhaled
        That drifted down and settling would cloy
Around the tasselled shade on her brass lamp,
                The single bulb it veiled
To prove love burns when feelings start to cool
Still fierce and bright and unconditional.

Not knowing how or where her love began
        I feel her fingertips retracing me
Their lathered reassurances, their span
           A soft idolatory
As, clenched inside this red lump of *Lifebuoy*,
Raw knuckles from her chapped and gold ringed hands,
Arthritic, shrinking, tighten to protect
        This slow and puzzled boy

Who, stepping from the bowl, misunderstands
                              The secrets that she kept
And how, emerged from what the past pretends,
Their altered truths, unspoken, come to cleanse.

A MILLION OF REPENTENCE

Dome cameras give CCTV
a glimpse, time-stamped, of what gods see,
fixed lenses rubbernecked to scan
the ways, if not the soul, of man,
at choke points where we too have rushed
through vents of warm, convected dust
up escalators, each inept
lead booted, myoclonic step
deliverance from, echoes spent,
cacophonies of what was meant
in tunnels tiled to shine and burn
down into time and time's return
while all that happens, happens twice
on plasma screens where pixels dice
with faces tilted, phone to phone,
gone down in pairs, come up alone,
or this street drinker hawking phlegm
who, shouting at an ATM,
stands tall as Special Brew allows
then sinks, dissolves into the crowd,
hears dead men cursing, mad crosstalk
through white tiled walls of sand and chalk,
through potash, permeable time,
where knee bones winter, tap roots climb,
as live rails over sleepers bring
lost poets back, propped up to sing
"how simplified our lives have grown
now they are yours that were our own,
conducted under cabled soil

while you make of them what you will,
and even as we failed and died
love charged us to outsource our pride,
commodify at their pin's fee
desire, ambition, vanity;
our dry bones play their waiting game
unrattled now its all the same
no matter who the blind roots crown
for who goes up and who goes down".

HYDRANGEAS
for Wendy

Pompoms of cultivars, mopheads, lacecaps,
Featherbrained, papery, filling a vase,
Lopped off before autumn's frosts and cold snaps
By green rubber gloves with sharp secateurs
And gathered together to jostle, impress
The ghosts of themselves with their colourfulness.

Turncoats, airheads in the dry-as-dust room,
Delicate boredoms where spiders once hung,
Alkaline, acid, each pink or blue bloom,
Cellular, spherical, weightless, homespun,
Hothoused and pampered, teased through the glass
By the long silver trail of a snail's slow trespass

That measures their fading, trapped behind nets
Or punished by sunshine blazing through chintz,
No longer our frou-frou pastel coquettes
But perms slowly loosing their brittle blue rinse
To tremble and nod as dusks test their weight
Or touched, scenting darkness, disintegrate.

A week in the window has left them too dry
To winter like us, too fragile and pale,
Dead heads, desiccated, a host to blackfly,
Propped up in the shed for cobwebs to veil,
Their watchful bereavements, their posthumous grace,
Bowed to the sunlight and dust they displace.

ÖTZI

Such changes in the climate changed his moods
And how he was, as changeable as weather,
Could vary at the higher altitudes
Where even pagan gods can't live forever.

Wait long enough and feelings cease to freeze,
Precipitate in alp and calving berg
Their primitive ice-age vocabularies
That melt and flood the world with cooler words.

So on a raft of bones he sailed between
The watersheds of North and South Tyrol,
Down Inn and Etsch, epoch and holocene,
Straight into all our human rigmarole.

Cold sealed his wounds, his sixty-one tattoos,
His helter-skelter through blind snow and ice,
His lungs displaced and breathless with bad news
Of arrowheads and human sacrifice.

Such troubles Ötzi, still such wild disputes,
All tumbled out defrosted from the past,
All down to you again, you old slyboots,
Dropped in once more to grin and flabbergast.

Ötzi, the natural mummy of a man from around 5,500 years ago, was discovered in 1991 in the Ötzal alps. Shifts in the landscape show that he may have died in what is now Austria although he was found 101 yards inside Italian territory. He was claimed and has been retained by Italy. The nature of his life and circumstances of his death have been the subject of much investigation and speculation.

ROUÉS

Where did they flee to? Who wrote off their debts
when, scuttled back into a gas mantled past,
they left just this pair of foxed silhouettes
inlayed to the depths of the shadows they cast?
Their off-cuts, spiralled and coiled to the floor,
were the shirts off their backs they left behind
for the brilliantined thief and the red-headed whore
who gave them the pox and robbed them both blind.

Brought out for the hanging, downlit, strung along
with woodcuts and etchings from last autumn's sale,
mocked by a stag's head knocked down for a song
they pose cock-a-hoop on a gold picture rail,
price-tagged in guineas, cockeyed with surprise,
sporting sold stickers, all set for their spree,
two *roués* quick scissorwork snipped and excised
now fallen among the *haute bourgeoisie*.

ON A BALCONY FALLING

Stripping off under a thin white towel
you wrung out your costume
and slung it over a tubular chair
so wantonly
it might, now empty, still be draining there,
spiralling lycra
into clear drops
that wobbled and fell
in long-stemmed chlorinations to the pool.

Today, tubed-up and shrunk
while a nurse checks on your drain,
you stir beneath the sheets
and your shape swims up again
from the white and red tiled oven
of a Tyrrhenian afternoon,
your tilt at the hip
as you turn to stare back
at me on a balcony falling,
headlong and drip by drip,
for the salt evaporations
of heelprints as they shrink
wherever heat will follow
in faint discipleship.

ONE FOR SORROW

An urban assembly of grey wheelie bins
lined up, handles out, down our dog-legged lane
and in one, dumped with giftwrap, bottles and tins,
weighed down by fake snow and a frail paperchain,
was our neighbour's upended Christmas tree,
its scatter of needles, crêpe and bent wire
and, crushed with a pop-up nativity,
baubleless branches still clasping their star,
still trailing light-fingered strands of lametta
slipstreamed by traffic on the school run,
all wriggling to show us how, tricky, quicksilver,
foil at its thieving pickpockets the sun
and snares with a cardboard, tinsel-crowned Christ
the magpie its larcenous glitter enticed.

GREENGAGE

Her tree still sheds it leaves, their fall
makes grief and grieving tangible,
and where a cast-iron drainpipe sleeves
rainwater poured from rotted eaves
an old grief, making water sing,
dies in the broken guttering,
and where her dormer window mists
she ghostwrites with her fingertips
or doodles breath as scrims of rain
bring gusts and squalls, stir up again
leaves falling through unfallen leaves
and this is how the greengage grieves.

ANOPHELES

Through trees, round rings in wood, time came and went.
Black minutes, in their gold half-hunter, flew.
A snowy owl shook out its soft lament
Unruffled by the foxes' ballyhoo,
While snails made cursive tracks, a silver scrawl
Across ragstone and brick, each squiggled line
A flourish in the writing on the wall
That proved our fictions nothing but moonshine.

Who climbed in here? Tin-snipped the chain-link fence?
Broke camp? Toe-poked the ashes of a fire?
Rolled dog-ends up to smoke out innocence?
Wiped off bad blood and skin from razor wire?
Anopheles, still sounding out suspects,
Whine on around the sweat glands in our necks.

A LATE CHRISTENING

A decade dead, still partying all night,
My parents bop and jive while I'm asleep
Or jitterbug through flickering blue light,
Emerging from dream footage in a blur
Of whispers, lies and secrets that, to keep,
They tissue-wrap in gossip as I stir,

Then hover among sisters with their gifts,
Who flirt, lit up by gin, wave cigarettes
In gold ringed hands and, tipsy, chance a kiss
Or later, by the kitchen sink, make eyes
At stainless ghosts a washed-up spoon reflects
And chrome with its mad silver magnifies.

Time settles in the ovals of teaspoons,
Age spots of tannin never quite removed
Evolving from worn coins to copper moons
Rinsed out yet ineradicably stained,
As if each burnish chemically proved
How love neglected turns to love engrained,

And so I've cleaned them up as offerings,
Bright charms against dark mornings and the loss
Of breath and scented polish where it clings
To names chased round a tarnished silver cup
By parents dawn has angered, time made cross,
Who leave and slam the door to wake me up.

SNOWBALL

She caught me as I played the fool
puffed up and gloved for our first fling,
her giggles shrill as icicles
hung from the school's white guttering,
then, soaking wet, we called a truce
by coat pegs in the corridor
where sleeves peeled back revealed the bruise
her dad said she'd been asking for.

In dreams I give the past a shake,
its snow, still virgin, powders moss,
dusts stones and licks of ice to cake
the school's iron railings rimed with frost
where one lost glove reached up to clutch
at gulls and clouds, snow-laundered things
so pure her dad could never touch
or, drunk, smear with his fingerings.

Wind combs the past for flurried clues
but turns up nothing more than snow,
lost hearts not knowing who stole whose
and bootprints still with miles to go
that break thin ice to prove moonlight
is not what it's cracked up to be
while stars at smash and grab incite
each dawn to daylight robbery.
Sometimes in bed the dream police
want samples of the blood and hair
of who got in and stripped the place
but left their footprints everywhere.

MUTE

Anger took a blowtorch to that summer
and wicked tongues turned blistered afternoons
to furnaces for temper tides left over
where midges, whining, tangled above dunes,
our casual rubbish tips filled with the spoil
from cheap self-medicated highs and lows,
popped blisterpacks, pill bottles, wraps of foil
ill winds and shifting sands might still expose.

Tonight though, on TV, as coffees cool,
our porous beach is littered with the drowned,
a soldier with a torch who finds a girl,
its beam, like love, leaves instantly spellbound,
or, motionless, a boy, his face rinsed clean,
still looking out to sea for his toy boat,
washed up inside our shallow plasma screen
you stare at as I reach for the Remote.

This could be us, our days of playing dead,
hungover, wasted, too young then to see
our luck that it was just ourselves we fled
not Homs, Fallujah, Raqqa, Tripoli,
and too late now to Pause or press Standby
or Mute and pay lip service to the drowned
with waves that wash a mouth out, roll an eye
our shame, in its new insolence, dumbfounds.

IODINE

Searching for names that now give her the slip
she jerks down the beach like a marionette,
wobbled by pebbles, propped on a stick,
wrapped up in cloud the mudflats reflect,
awkwardly trying to fathom a tide
as it freezes soft tissue and, burning, withdraws
what's left of the past scraped out from inside
with sponges, dead jellyfish, tentacles, claws
that float, amniotic, and for pity's sake,
draw her back in for the waves to deep clean,
delivered once more of her *little mistake*
by the screams of the gulls and the sea's iodine.

Coming back up through the empty sunbeds,
she pulls on black leggings, dabs at chilblains,
disheartened at how blood purples and threads
spider-like now through a dozen new veins
squeezed into heels as the afternoon goes
with breezes and clouds and, chilled in their shade,
all of the sunlight an old body owes
to the girl she once was for a summer mislaid.

SHOO

Ball-bearings, silver, tilted in
his lidless gold tobacco tin
tip out and strike the garage floor
like props dropped by a conjuror
who scrabbles for them in the dark
blackthreaded by the scent of bark
to feel, in earth caked on a spade,
the soul his careless ghost mislaid
slip through cold hands that disinter
the winter bulbs he left for her,
while cobwebs, hung on filthy glass,
cling to him when she brushes past,
count off in beads of autumn rain
full moons as they roll round again
and tremble with her breathing in
the stir of dust shed by his skin.

This time he's back to rattle locks,
knock spanners in their steel toolbox,
wear shadow as a widow's peak
to play dusk's game of hide-and-seek
with spirit level, bob and line,
evaporations, turpentine
on rag torn from a summer dress
she comes tonight to repossess,
shook out with rust and moth to wipe
his monkey wrench and copper pipe
and dust enough to shoo him in
the shine inside his empty tin.

CHIN UP

He'd reached the wood scrubbed up and clean,
still drinking as a late sun flared
on windows like acetylene
as if the dusk could be repaired,
while further in, turned submarine,
thick shrubs clung to a footpath where
he passed out as the pills kicked in,
a dead man in cheap summerwear
among the crows that kept an eye
on all such things that fall behind
the wood's last bits of tattered sky
snapped shut in its ramshackle blind.

Dried berries, ivy, roots and stones
were mixed up with him long before
a fox on heat nosed out his bones,
a cold snap broke his brittle jaw
swung open now to grin at flies
or, chin up, take a swig of rain
before the tides of bluebells rise
and, sober, he goes down again.

SINGALONG

Lit up and out of tune she'd bawl
to make her ten green bottles fall,
but near the end, its song and dance,
they came down like an avalanche;
decades of empties drained and tossed
in stairwells, basements, cellars, lost
to blackouts or, pulled back once more,
this locked ward off a corridor
it took a white gowned summer
of heat and gauze to wheel her down.

Dried out by autumn, washed and dressed,
she'd idled into brittleness,
stick-thin with rage, with nicotine,
the doped rice paper of her skin
too yellow now, too old, too wrong
to bottlebank a singalong
or raise, hoarse from its shattered past,
through lacerations of smashed glass,
her voice again, uproarious.

CLOCK & THISTLE

He'd holed up in a mildewed flowerpot,
the torn out leather tongue from her lost shoe
or weather-beaten uppers left to rot,
indulging his *nostalgie de la boue*,
too petrified to jump out of his skin
or blink to see, before the light should die,
her summer's silks and colours perished in
these powdered bits of moth and butterfly.

Clearing out their shed I find her cane
to tap into the darkness, make a stir,
unnerved as he leaps back to life again
among the scattered husks I disinter,
old vanities, dry seasons, sunlight blown
with brittle wing tips weightless as permed hair
through dusty reclamations of limestone
left over from her castles in the air,

their cloud-topped turrets tumbled to white rock
heaped up behind a ruined wishing well
while, riotous with toadflax, lady's smock,
her stepping stones lay broken where they fell,
and where, beneath a lamp to light him home,
got up in fresh chalk paint to play the fool,
still fishing for old boots, her plaster gnome
survives unscathed by all but ridicule

made hollow by the last of her footprints
that skirt their dried out pond, escorting me,
the frog who never quite became a prince,
back through her weeds, her paths, her rockery;
all gone to seed, to clock and thistle blown
on notes a blackbird scores with thorn and rake
to piercingly unearth an old ringtone
and, feathers ruffled, give her dust a shake.

IN A NUTSHELL

A walnut splits and cracks in half
spinning like a coracle
through tea lights on a green oilcloth
then rocks and clatters to a hollow stop.
This evening, and while candles burn,
its wrinkled lining might contain
my mother's stitched and shrivelled skin,
thin shoulder blades dipped to a wave,
gold foil her fee for ferrying
around old corks and dark wine spills
a mad girl to the other side,
astonished it is her, that she has died.

Annoyed, lips pursed, she holds her tongue,
its silver coin, long obsolete,
is loose change now and rolled away
for Furies to collect as she,
returned in rags the years have left,
is unpicked like embroidery
shook out with hornet, beetle, moth,
then shredded by cracked fingernails
in dusty sleeves of torn sackcloth
and pulverized with bone and shell,
their fragments, scattered on her breath,
all rattling down to wake us up
by half-light in the small hours with
wingless husks of panic and surprise.

OYSTER THIEF

Should we, dear ghost, by chance once more,
through long exhaustions, touch again
and, hand in hand still, comb the shore
for oyster thief or lion's mane

I might, light-fingered at low tide,
skim pebbles, lift a mermaid's purse,
or pilfer starfish calcified
where clouds of thunderflies disperse

on turning waves poured in to swell
their shallows as a crab sidesteps
a nicked, flicked-open razor-shell
the glint of sunlit gravel whets

to shred its foam, its grubby lace
that tatters mud, cold shoulders stones,
loops necklaces of jellyfish
for you who never made old bones,

but steal back now, as I nod off,
and pick your way down to the sea
through rock pools cold and deep enough
to wash, once more, your hands of me.